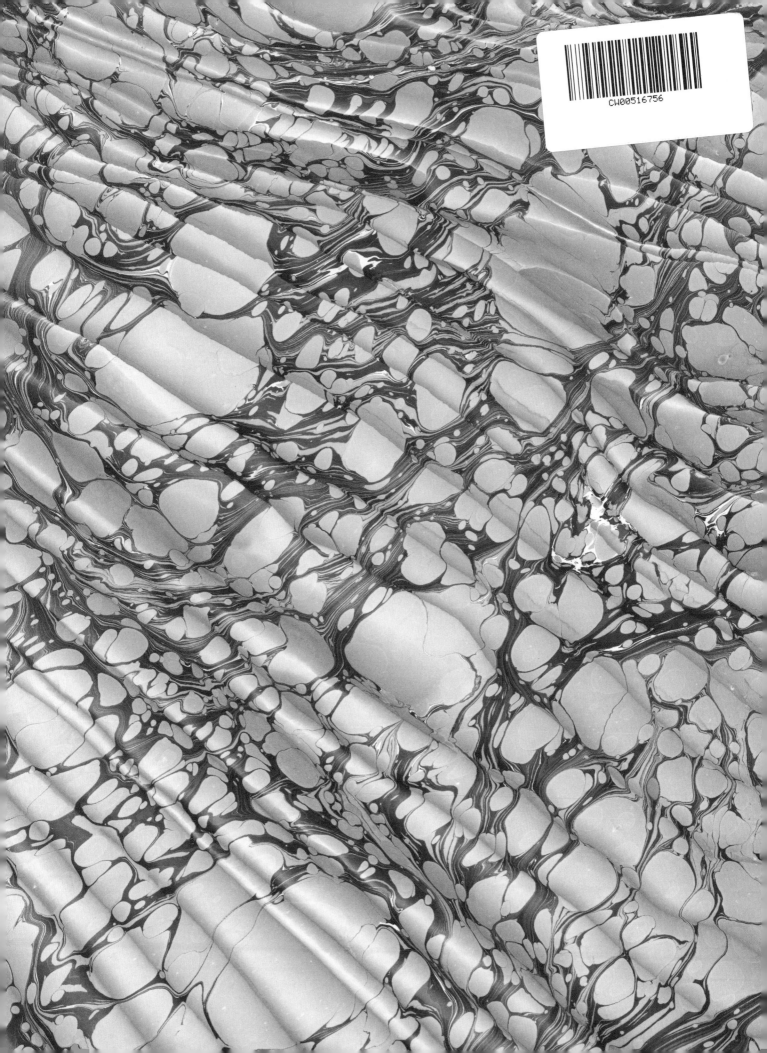

BOW ACCESSORIES

Equipment and Trimmings You Can Make

BOW ACCESSORIES
EQUIPMENT AND TRIMMINGS YOU CAN MAKE

VOLKMAR HÜBSCHMANN (ed.)

Schiffer Publishing Ltd

4880 Lower Valley Road, Atglen, Pennsylvania 19310

Bow Accessories—
Equipment and Trimmings you can make

Editor	Volkmar Hübschmann
Authors	Volker Alles
	Andrea & Uwe Gangnus
	Ekkehard Höhn
	Volkmar Hübschmann
	Georg Klöss
	Jürgen Knöll
	Herbert Müller
	Willi Müller
	Heinrich Prell
	Michael Prinz
	Stefan Schwed
Cover photo	Volker Alles
Layout	Birgit Eicher, Angelika Hörnig
Collaboration	Joey Frosch, Bernhard Hölzl

Translated by Dr. Edward Force, Central Connecticut State University

Copyright © 2008 by Schiffer Publishing, Ltd.
Library of Congress Control Number: 2008927637

Originally published as Bogenschiessen: Ausrüstung und Zubehör selbst gemacht by VERLAG ANGELIKA HÖRNIG

Designed by "Sue"
Type set in Sans Ex/Zurich BT

ISBN: 978-0-7643-3035-3
Printed in China

Schiffer Books are available at special discounts for bulk purchases for sales promotions or premiums. Special editions, including personalized covers, corporate imprints, and excerpts can be created in large quantities for special needs. For more information contact the publisher:

Published by Schiffer Publishing Ltd.
4880 Lower Valley Road
Atglen, PA 19310
Phone: (610) 593-1777; Fax: (610) 593-2002
E-mail: Info@schifferbooks.com

For the largest selection of fine reference books on this and related subjects, please visit our web site at **www.schifferbooks.com**
We are always looking for people to write books on new and related subjects. If you have an idea for a book please contact us at the above address.

This book may be purchased from the publisher.
Include $5.00 for shipping.
Please try your bookstore first.
You may write for a free catalog.

In Europe, Schiffer books are distributed by
Bushwood Books
6 Marksbury Ave.
Kew Gardens
Surrey TW9 4JF England
Phone: 44 (0) 20 8392-8585; Fax: 44 (0) 20 8392-9876
E-mail: info@bushwoodbooks.co.uk
Website: www.bushwoodbooks.co.uk
Free postage in the U.K., Europe; air mail at cost.

Foreword

Holding a good book in my hands is still for me—even in the days of the electronic media—a very pleasant feeling.

Whoever seeks information on particular subjects nowadays often goes to the Internet first. The wealth of information offered there is in many cases vast, and varies from outstanding to fully useless, even misleading and false.

Naturally, information and instructions are also available in printed form that contain errors or need correction. In my experience, though, the quality of information in a specialist book is, as a rule, considerably higher than colorfully thrown-together information, tips, and experiences from the Internet.

Even though it was not always easy to assemble the contents of this book, still it was a pleasant feeling to know that, over time, the original collection of themes grew into an impressive pile of manuscripts. It has given me a great deal of pleasure to describe all those work processes, techniques, materials and tools that are required for the creation of the most varied objects.

Because of the relatively large numbers of authors who have cooperated on this book, a large part of the knowledge and experience needed to create one's own traditional equipment, except for the bow, can be found here. This knowledge is now assembled and preserved for the future in the form of a book.

This book became possible only through the cooperation of the numerous authors, all of whom were ready to share their knowledge and ability. I would like to thank every single one of them most heartily at this point!

My thanks also go out to those people who have contributed indirectly to the creation of this book by directing me to people with special capabilities. Likewise to all who were of help with the photographic and written documentation and stood at my side to deal with my questions in word and deed.

Volkmar Hübschmann
Mannheim, Autumn 2006

Contents

Foreword _____ 5

Why make equipment yourself? _____ 9

Equipment

Tooled leather armguard _____ 12

Stone-Age bone armguard _____ 20

Shooting gloves and tabs _____ 22

Belt pouch _____ 26

Arrow-seeking hook _____ 27

Archers' knives _____ 28

Tassels _____ 34

Bow-stringing cord _____ 35

Quivers

Thoughts about quivers _____ 40

Tooled back quiver _____ 42

Back quiver with built-in knife sheath _____ 44

St. Charles quiver _____ 50

Oetzi quiver made of felt _____ 55

Hip quiver in Plains Indian style _____ 62

Tooled hip quiver _____ 68

Holster quiver _____ 71

Other quiver types _____ 74

Arrow Shafts

Preliminary information _____ 80

The self-notch _____ 82

Spine-testers _____ 84

Arrow-repair splices _____ 88

Tapering of shafts _____ 90

Tapering in practice _____ 92

Making arrow shafts _____ 94

Arrow straightener _____ 103

Shaft working _____ 104

Painting arrows with Lego _____ 108

Wrapping arrows _____ 115

Leather broadhead _____ 118

Contents

Feathering Arrows

Basics of feathering arrows _____ 124
Materials and tools for feathering _____ 126
Building your own feathering device_____ 130
Cutting feathers _____ 134
Feather burners _____ 138
De luxe feathering _____ 142
Flu-Flu arrows_____ 150
Tracers _____ 156

Bowstrings

Gallows for Flemish plaited strings _____ 160
A Flemish plaited string _____ 162
Endless string _____ 167
Central wrapping and nocking point _____ 171
String silencer_____ 173
String holder _____ 174
String wax _____ 175

Targets

A simple target standard _____ 178
Animal targets made of foam _____ 179
Special targets and moving targets_____ 186

Other

Horn, antler and bone _____ 198
Building your own workbench_____ 201
A shooting chair _____ 206

Authors and Artisans

_____ 208

Appendix

Literature to take you farther _____ 212
English units of measurement _____ 214

Why Make Equipment Yourself?

Whoever would like to practice traditional archery at the present time is confronted by a rich assortment of equipment items.

As with bows themselves, the archer has a choice from all imaginable industrially produced and so-called "custom-made" accessories. The latter are usually individual pieces, made according to the customer's wishes and needs. This type of production is reflected in the quality and prices of goods made by serious artistic artisans.

Many traditional archers are also inclined to make at least a part of their equipment themselves. The reason for this is not necessarily the financial savings, for these are often balanced by hours of devoted handicraft, but rather the wish for unmistakable, very personal equipment.

Giving one's own creativity a free hand, creating things with one's own hands that correspond fully to one's own conceptions and needs, this is the real reason that leads to doing it yourself. The finished object and the work itself provide joy. It is a good feeling to do one's own work while completely wrapped up in one's own ideas. From my personal experience I know that one can forget time and space all too easily.

At present there is a whole series of good books on the subject of bow building, in which the making of accessories is only described more or less secondarily. This book is meant to close those gaps and concentrate exclusively on the accessories, thus serving as an advisor and source of inspiration for making one's own equipment.

Everyone who has some handcrafting ability and a small basic stock of tools and materials can thus experience the difference between "self-made" and merely bought.

Lots of luck and great success in your work!

Volkmar Hübschmann

Equipment for the Archer

Tooled leather armguard

Stone-Age bone armguard

Shooting glove and tab

Belt pouch

Arrow-seeking hook

Archers' knives

Tassels

Bow-stringing cord

Tooled Leather Armguard

Leatherwork: Joey Frosch; text and photos: Volkmar Hübschmann

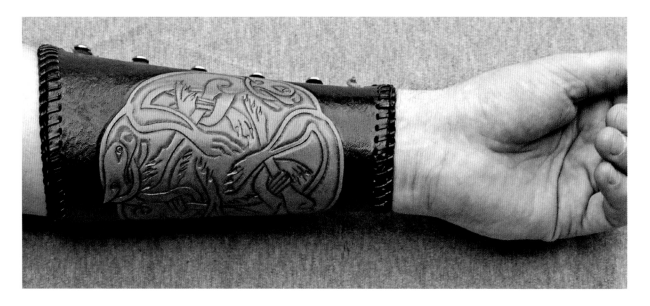

An armguard protects the forearm from the bowstring as it snaps forward.
Whoever has absent-mindedly let his unprotected forearm come into contact with the bowstring will not forget this very uncomfortable experience very soon, and will gladly wear an armguard in the future.

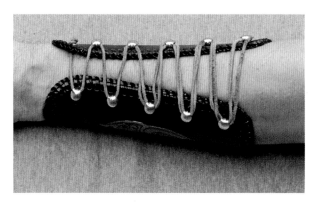

An armguard can be made of various materials and take various forms. Widespread and well proved in practice are leather armguards with hooks of the kind that one finds, for example, on hiking boots.

Along with the instructions for such a padded armguard, the basic techniques of decorating the leather and binding the edges will be portrayed.

The leather used is plain, natural leather from cattle, also called belt leather.

A leather piece measuring about 25 x 25 centimeters, with a thickness of 3 mm, is needed.

One can make his own cardboard model from the pattern shown here or invent his own pattern. The type shown below can easily be adapted to the individual arm shape and length.

Before the leather is cut, make sure that the armguard fits well.

The armguard should extend from the wrist—about where a wristwatch is worn—to about 6 cm before the elbow joint. At the front, the width of the armguard represents the circumference of the wrist; at the rear, that of the forearm.

The circumferences are measured on the unclothed arm. If clothing is worn under the armguard in colder weather, the difference can be equalized by the lacing.

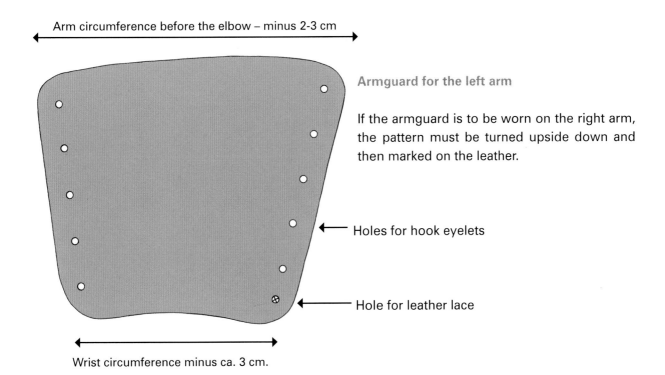

Arm circumference before the elbow – minus 2-3 cm

Armguard for the left arm

If the armguard is to be worn on the right arm, the pattern must be turned upside down and then marked on the leather.

Holes for hook eyelets

Hole for leather lace

Wrist circumference minus ca. 3 cm.

The needed tools are:
- Marble plate as tooling surface
- Tooling hammer and heavier hammer
- Hole pipes
- Hole iron for plaited belts, single/multiple
- Plaiting needle
- Cutting knife, half-moon knife
- Steel ruler
- Leather shears
- Swivel-knife
- Angle breaker
- Modeling tool

With the pointed end of the modeling tool, one first traces the outline of the pattern and the holes for the eyelets for the leather lacing.

Then the armguard is cut out, using the cutting knife and the shears.

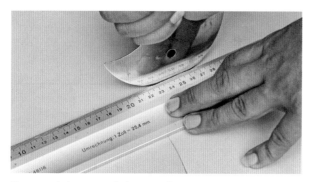

For straight cuts, it is good to cut along the edge of a steel ruler.
Curves and narrow roundings are better cut with the swivel-knife, so as to cut them finally with the shears.

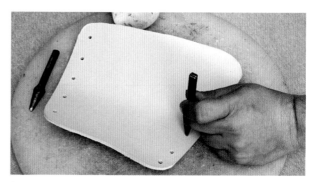

In the properly cut armguard, the holes for the hooks or eyelets are now punched with the hole pipe, using a cutting board as a working surface.

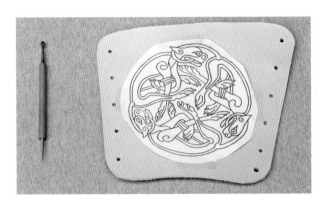

The armguard is now finished to the point at which the tooling can begin.

Step 1
Place the motif pattern on the leather and fix it at several points with strips of tape.

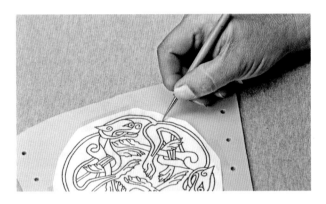

Step 2
Transfer the lines (contours) of the motif by pressing gently on the leather with the pointed end of the modeling tool.

Step 3
Now cut the transferred lines in with the swivel-knife.

Tooled Leather Armguard

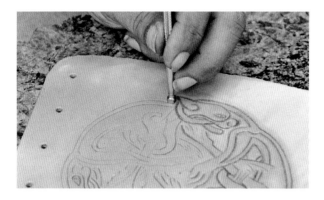

Step 4

Now the leather is dampened evenly on both sides with a wet sponge and then tooled along the already cut lines. (Beveler B 986 or B 198)

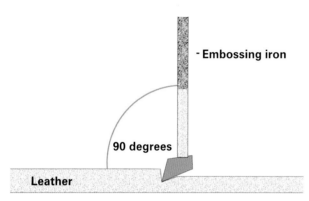

- Embossing iron

90 degrees

Leather

Step 5

With the spoon-shaped end of the modeling tool, press in or go over the tooled lines.

Step 6

With the tooling iron (A 114), the background is formed.

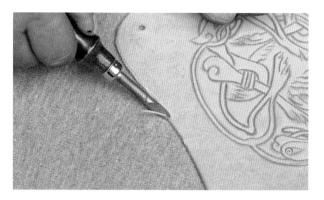

The actual tooling is finished after this job.
It is important that one have a spatial concept in order to be able to create three-dimensional relief-like motifs.

When the leather is thoroughly dry, one prepares all the edges around the edge of the armguard with the angle-breaker.

The armguard is now ready to be painted.
With a brush and special leather paint, the armguard is painted black around the motif.

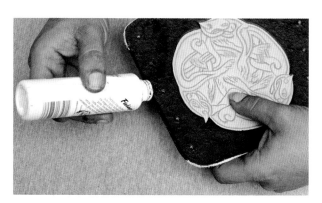

The edges can be painted with an angle colorer (a plastic bottle with a sponge under the cap).

The actual motif is colored with special wiped-on paint. This paint (shadowing colors) is best applied with a damp sponge, using circling motions.
After one or two minutes, one wipes off the excess paint with a clean sponge and clear water.
The coloring with wiped-on paint heightens the plastic effect.

Tooled Leather Armguard

When all the paint has dried, the hooks and the eyes for the leather lacing can be riveted with the riveting machine.

Whoever does not have a riveting machine can go to a shoemaker, if he can be of help, or if one cannot find a shoemaker, to a saddler.

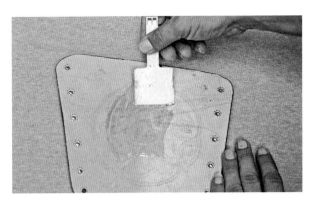

To line the armguard, the back is coated with contact cement (with a small spatula).

And then a piece of dyed deer leather is glued onto the back.

As soon as the glue has sealed, the excess deer leather is cut off along the edges of the armguard.

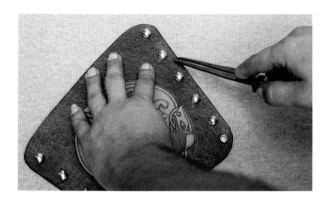

When all the paint has dried, the hooks and the eyes for the leather lacing can be riveted with the riveting machine.

Whoever does not have a riveting machine can go to a shoemaker, if he can be of help, or if one cannot find a shoemaker, to a saddler.

To line the armguard, the back is coated with contact cement (with a small spatula).

And then a piece of dyed deer leather is glued onto the back.

As soon as the glue has sealed, the excess deer leather is cut off along the edges of the armguard.

Stone-Age Bone Armguard

Volker Alles

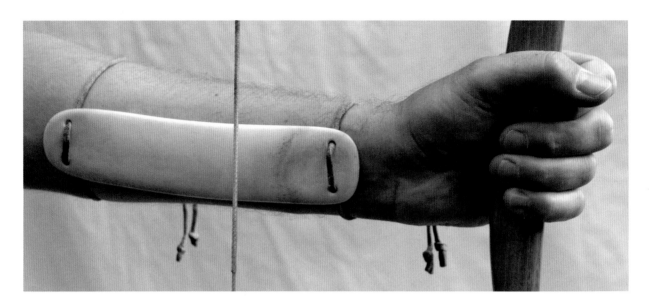

Forearm protection exists in as many forms as there are archery cultures, and practically everything that was available and usable has been used, from old strips of cloth to the classiest materials.

The leather armguard worn today by most archers is probably a very recent invention, but many arm protectors have been devised in the form of a plate or strip of various materials, and in a variety of forms, from very simple to richly decorated.

In the heat of the summer, though, it can become unpleasantly hot under such a leather armguard.

For this reason, I got the idea of making myself a light and airy armguard that would fit in visually with my Stone-Age equipment.

So I asked the butcher for a big, tubular cooked-out bone, without joint ends, but not yet sawn into pieces.

This bone has a cross-section that is highly arched on one side and flat on the other. Because of its slightly curved shape, it can well be used as forearm protection. It is best to obtain several bones at once (left and right legs) and try them out to see which one fits one's arm best. These bones can then be cooked out intensively again or bleached, as you wish (see the "Horn, Antler and Bone" chapter). I wanted it to be thoroughly natural and thus decided not to use bleach.

With a bandsaw, I cut the bone longitudinally along its flat side and rounded the two ends. With rather coarse toothing and not too fast cutting, one prevents the saw blade from getting clogged with bone meal or overheating. Pushing forward too fast should also be avoided, for bone is rather hard and a burden for any saw blade.

The same principle also applies to rasping, which is used for further working: Finely toothed iron files get clogged right away and become unusable. Important above all is that one gets a cabinet or half-round rasp, so that one has both a flat and a rounded side.

With the flat side, the edges remaining from the sawing are removed and the bone plate is worked at all the edges; with the curved side, one can now deepen the natural curve on the inside of the bone, so that the armguard fits the forearm well. Above all, the bone is so thick in the middle that one can remove some more material there.

At each and of the armguard plate, drill two 4 mm holes. Then remove the still-visible scratches from the rasp work with coarse sandpaper. One should not go over it to get especially fine grainings, for bone, when it is not totally leached chemically, has the practical quality of polishing itself from constant use and, in time, acquiring a nice smooth, lightly glowing surface.

Whoever wants to can now decorate his armguard with Stone-Age scratched drawings and make the grooves visible with coloring, such as water-insoluble drawing ink.

For attachment to the arm, one only needs two strips of leather and two suitable beads.

I cut the leather strips, of about 2 x 4 mm thickness, out of a piece of chamois-tanned deer leather. For the pearls I used leftover pieces of bone, for a big piece of bone has such a thick wall in the middle that one can easily make two bone beads, some 12-14 mm thick, out of it.

The borehole should be of such a small diameter that one can just slide the leather strips in by hand, but should appear to be much too small for two leather strips.

Since the bead should serve as a variable closing, it has to be hard to move on the doubled leather strip. In addition to the authentic appearance, this is the main reason for the soft chamois leather, for the beef-leather strips you can buy are too soft to be used.

One inserts the leather strips through the two holes at each end of the bone plate, then one end through the bead; then one cuts the other end so that it tapers to its tip.

This thinned end is then placed on the other end of the leather strip just before the bead. If the hole in the bead is very tight, one can stick the ends together there with adhesive.

Then one pulls on the thick end, and the thin end is pulled through the bead with it. Each end is knotted, so that we do not absent-mindedly pull the leather out of the bead.

To put the armguard on, one puts his forearm through both pairs of leather strips and moves the bead with the other hand until the armguard is lying against the forearm.

To remove it, slide the beads to the end knots, and now one can slip one's arm out of the armguard.

If the leather strips are long enough, such an armguard will also fit over heavy winter clothing.

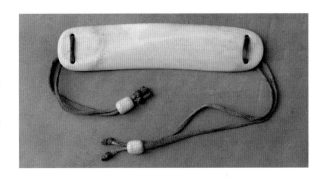

Shooting Gloves and Tabs

Leatherwork: Joey Frosch and Volkmar Hübschmann. Text and photos: Volkmar Hübschmann

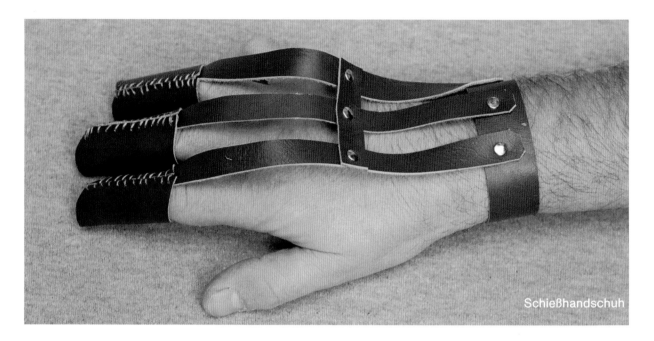

Schießhandschuh

A shooting glove or tab protects the fingers of the shooting hand. Releasing the arrow without wearing a glove can be a painful situation.

Whether you use a shooting glove or a tab is up to you.
It is best to try both and then decide on the basis of which protection suits you better.

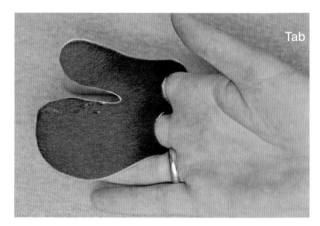

Tab

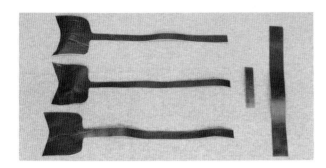

A shooting glove can easily be made at home (using leather needles). The leather should be stable but not too thick (about 1.5 mm), and have a smooth outside.

Step 1

Using the cutting pattern (see the sketch on the next page), the three finger caps with the holding belts, the belt for the back of the hand, and the belt for the wrist can be cut out.
The size of the caps must be individually fitted to the size of the fingers.
The caps are sewed together above the fingernails. The holding belt runs under the seam, inside the cap, to the wrist.

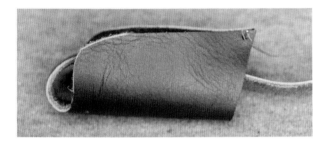

The belts are 12 mm wide and, depending on hand size, some 20-25 cm long.

Step 2

After the caps have been sewed and all the belts fitted to the individual hand size, the individual parts are riveted together with six small hollow rivets.

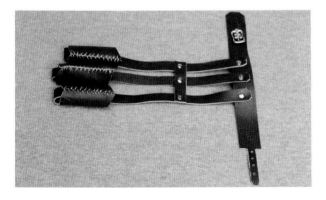

Step 3

To attach the wrist belt, one can use a small buckle or—not quite so traditionally—a strip of velcro.

The shooting glove should always be well treated with leather grease, so that it stays soft and comfortable.

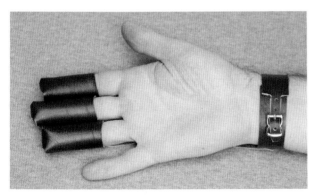

A tab can be made easily out of leather or some other suitable hide. The leather can be somewhat heavier than that of a shooting glove, and should be as smooth as possible, thus not veined.

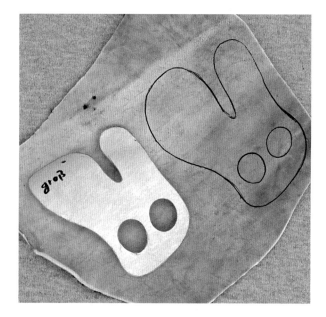

Step 1

The cutting pattern of the tab is transferred to stiff paper.

(Naturally, one can also make tabs with just one hole for the middle finger, or with three holes.) By using this paper tab, one determines the needed size and the diameter of the finger holes. The tab must cover the fingertips when they hold the bowstring, but should not reach out beyond them.

Step 2

The outlines of the fitted paper tab are now transferred to the leather or hide and cut out. Finally, all the edges should be smoothed with a piece of sandpaper.

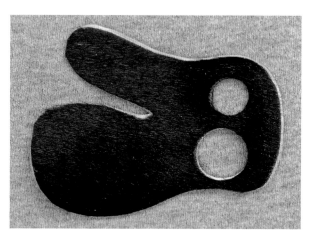

For a hide tab (the one shown here is made of horsehide), the direction in which the hair grows must absolutely be noted.

The bowstring slides over the tab in the same direction as the hairs.

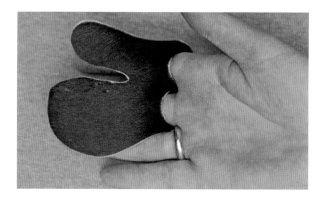

Naturally, the tab should also be treated regularly, so that the leather does not get hard and brittle.

The pattern

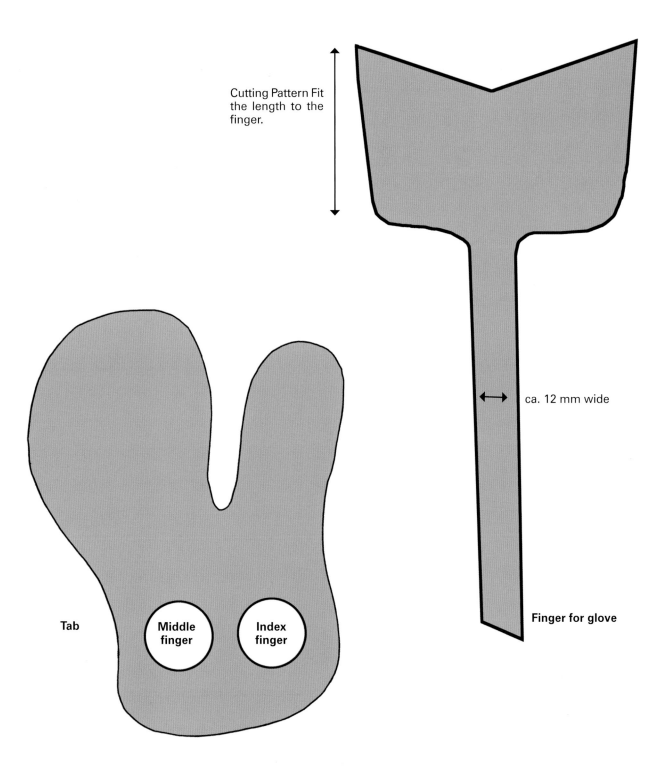

Cutting Pattern Fit
the length to the
finger.

ca. 12 mm wide

Tab

**Middle
finger**

**Index
finger**

Finger for glove

Belt Pouch

Leatherwork: Joey Frosch; text and photos, Volkmar Hübschmann

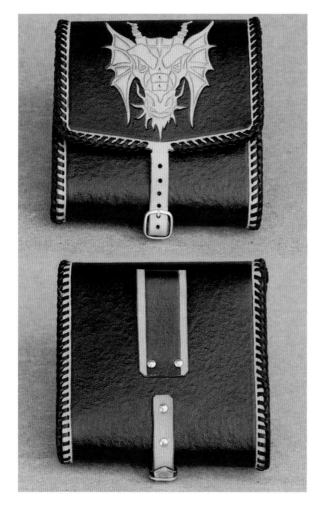

A belt pouch makes sense particularly in the warmer part of the year, when one goes around without a jacket and thus has fewer pockets in which to stow small objects.

There are, after all, a few things that an archer in action should always have with him. They include a shot-in spare bowstring, pliers or a multi-tool, spare points, glue, a pen, bandages, handkerchiefs, or even a container for food.

If one grows accustomed to carrying these things with him always in a container made especially for them, then they are always at hand when needed.

The pouch shown here is 17 cm high, 16.5 cm wide and 4 cm deep. The pattern is relatively simple and can be copied from the illustrations and cut out easily.

When all the work, such as tooling, coloring and making holes along the edges, is finished, the loop for the belt and the strap with the buckle can be riveted on.

Then the edges can be wrapped and the two identical side parts bound together.

Arrow-Seeking Hook

Volkmar Hübschmann

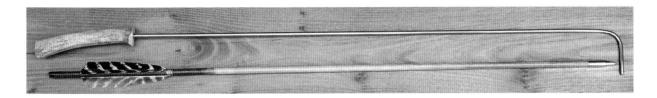

Who is not familiar with this: an arrow has just whizzed past the target and is now somewhere in the grass, in the open woods.

The most suitable tool for the search for such arrows is a seeking hook, which is also known as a scratcher. Building such an arrow-seeking hook is relatively simple.

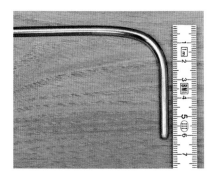

The staff should definitely be made of spring steel, so that despite the pressure of being used for seeking, it will always spring back to its original straight form and not remain bent permanently.

A piece of spring steel one meter long, with a diameter of 5 mm, can be obtained for a low price at a model and hobby shop.

So that no sharp bend results, the end of the rod is bent about 90 degrees in a vise over a pipe at a length of about 6 cm, and rounded in hemispherical form.

Next one needs a handle. This can be a tool handle, a piece of wood or antler—whatever is on hand.

A piece of antler serves as the handle of my arrow-seeking hook and lies in the hand very well. A hole with the diameter of the rod and a depth of 8 to 10 cm is drilled in the handle.

Then the spring-steel rod is cut to length. The scratcher can have approximately the length of an arrow. The shorter the scratcher, the lighter it is, and the easier to transport. With a somewhat longer scratcher, of course, it is easier to seek. Here everyone decides for himself as to what length he decides on. A total length of some 60 cm has proved to be a good compromise for me.

When the steel rod is cut to length, it is pointed on a grinder and roughened at the end where it is glued into the handle.

Archers' Knives

Volkmar Hübschmann

For most archers it goes without saying that one carries a knife in the field. First of all, archers need a knife to cut arrows out of trees, branches, targets, etc. (This should not be taken as an invitation to do nature more damage than is absolutely necessary!) Also for all tasks that occur in camping.

If one takes a closer look at these knives, one notices that the bigger, firmer knives are generally hunting knives. Of course hunting knives are primarily cutting tools.

Thus everyone who uses a blade as a lever risks breaking off the tip or, at worst, the whole blade—depending on the qualities of the material and the shape of the blade.

In my view, a so-called camp knife is a better choice for non-hunting archers.

In a knife catalog I noticed a knife that I believe optimally meets the needs of an archer who does not hunt. This is the *Hirschkrone Piloten/SEK Messer*.

It looks very much like the well-known *Puma White Hunter*; the blade and handle lengths and the type of steel (German Workshop Number 1.4116) are identical.

A special demand made on the blade of the pilot knife is that a jet fighter pilot, if necessary, can pry with the knife if the explosive charges that are to blow off the canopy (ejector seat) fail.

This quality was attained by special hardening of the 5 mm thick, rust-free blade. The hardness at the tip of the blade is some 57 RC and decreases to about 51 RC to the handle. This gives it a flexibility of 15% at the handle.

The knife is available with three different blade types (smooth back, axe blade and saw-tooth) and various handles (wood, deer antler, Micarta, hard rubber).

The blades, the hollow rivets of the handle (aluminum or brass), small tubes for strap snaps, and various handle materials can also be obtained individually. Thus they are an interesting alternative for people who assemble their knives themselves or want to design their own.

I order blades with saw-tooth backs, brass inner handles, five (two as spares) brass hollow rivets and one snap tube. I already had a piece of Bubinga wood for the handle panels.

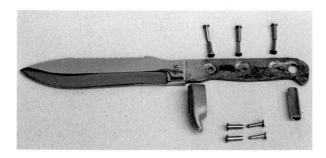

When I first examined the ready-made blade, I noticed the good workmanship of it. The transition from the blade to the crosspiece was exact and symmetrical, the blade was neatly ground (not sharply tapered) and well polished. No further work could be seen on the blade itself except that of tapering the cutting edge more, to give the blade its true sharpness.

The brass guard was in the condition that it came out of the mold, rough and not smoothed.

First the blade was wrapped heavily with tape from the blade to the crossbar.

That serves first to prevent injury, and second, it also protects the blade from damage while attaching it.

The blade was simply hardened after leaving the drop forge. Thus the side surfaces of the plate were first smoothed with a file (keep it at right angles!), and the contour of the piece was filed precisely.

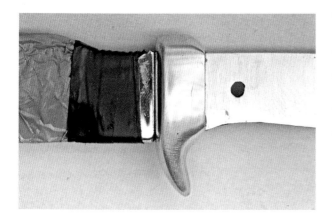

When the surface has its final form, then work the guard.

The casting ridges must be removed and the rough surface made smooth. The front of the guard (up to the blade) is now given its final polished surface.

Then the inside of the guard is worked with key files, so that it fits tightly and play-free on the tang.

Now the inner surfaces of the shoulder and the tang are degreased with acetone and coated with epoxy. (Be sure to wipe off excess epoxy at once!) After the adhesive has dried, the handle is filed into its final form; then the traces of the file are removed with sandpaper.

From a scrap of Bubinga wood I sawed two small boards measuring 120 x 40 x 12 mm, as a pair of panels for the handle.

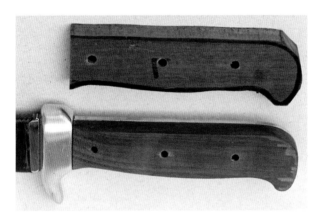

Using the tang as a pattern, I transferred the handle shape to the wood, sawed it out with a bandsaw and rasped it roughly into shape (no exactly on the line, leaving the grip panels slightly larger). Then I marked the grip panels with "left" and "right" and then marked the holes for the rivets, using the tang as the pattern for them.

In the next step, the grip panels received their almost final shape, which required a clean, split-free seat on the tng and at the transition to the shoulder.

In making the knife, I decided to omit the hole for the catch-strap snap.

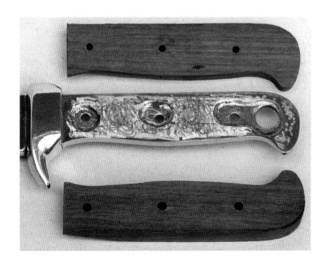

When everything fits together well, the gluing surfaces of the tang are slightly abraded (with a Dremel grinder using a tapered stone) and all gluing surfaces are degreased with acetone. In the next step, the grip panels are neatly and individually glued to the tang with epoxy.

The rivets served as holders in this process, but were removed again after the grip panels had been fixed with small screw clamps.

Excess glue in the rivet holes and on the edges must be removed at once!

When the grip panels are glued, the grip receives its final form (round the edges; the grip can be a little thicker in the center and have a bulbous form), and the holes for the rivets are sunk on each side. Before the actual riveting, put a drop of epoxy in each rivet hole.

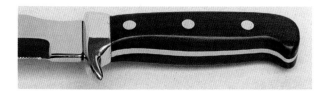 

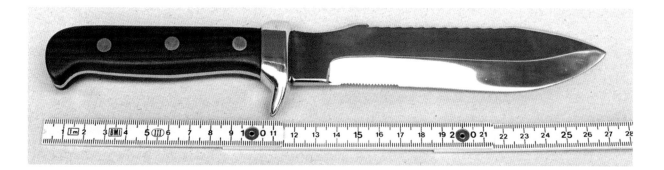

The knife is now finished to the point that it can receive its final form and finish (polish). I have sealed the grip panels several times with hard-oil and then polished them with parquet wax. All metal surfaces in the grip area were polished to a high gloss.

Since I do not want either designs or lettering on knives, it pleased me that the "SEK" trade mark could be polished out quite easily.

The double row of saw-teeth on my knife give good service in a makeshift manner, though they are far inferior to a real saw.

The knife is now finished; now one can devote oneself to the sheath.

The Knife Sheath

Because of the pronounced guard element, one cannot sew a quiver sheath for this knife. The best choice, in my opinion, is a belt sheath, in which the knife is secured by a strap running diagonally over the shoulder with a snap button.

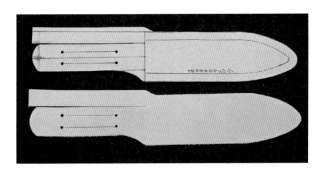

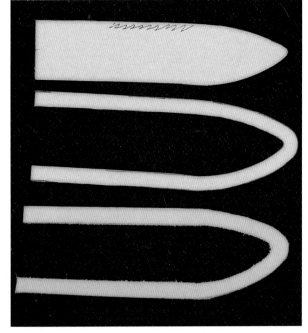

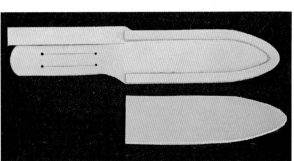

First I drew the outline of the blade up to the shoulder on a sheet of cardboard {note that the widest part of the blade applies to the sheath along the entire length of the blade!). Around this outline I allowed about one centimeter for stitching; thus arose the external form of the sheath in the blade area.

At the top, the sheath is continued with the leather straps for fastening the sheath to the belt, and the securing strap.

With a cardboard pattern, I determined the outline of the sheath. When the pattern is worked out to this extent, it serves as a pattern for the cutting of the leather. The cutout piece of leather forms the back of the sheath.

Now the upper part of the cardboard pattern is cut out, and in fact right where the shoulder begins. From the lower part of the pattern, the blade shape (note the widest part!) is cut out. Thus one gets a frame about a centimeter wide.

This frame is glued to the back of the sheath with contact cement, and the frame may need to be made of several layer of leather, until it has reached a thickness that is just a little less than the thickness of the blade.

On the front piece, the sunken stitch line is cut out and the holes made with an awl.

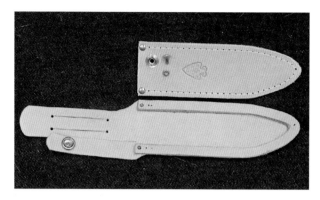

If the front is to be decorated, stamped or tooled, then this must be done now, as well as the riveting of the lower part of the snap button.

When the front is finished, it is glued onto the frame. Then all the holes that were marked are made with the all, absolutely vertical and all the way through.
At the beginning and at the end of the stitching, a hole is made for a rivet.

So that the stitching does not get worn from use, it must be sunk on the front and back; thus the leather is cut into with a stitch-sinker.
Additional protection is provided by rivets to the right and left of the blade opening.
After the sheath has beevn glued, stitched and riveted, one can put the knife in, fit the securing strap, and rivet on the top piece of the snap button.

Finally, the slits through which the belt will be passed are cut, all angles are smoothed, and finally the entire sheath is rubbed several times with leather grease.

If problems should occur with the riveting, especially with the snap button, a friendly shoemaker or saddler can certainly help.

More information on the described knife can be had from the firm of Rudolf Weber, Jr. (see sources in appendix).

Tassels

Volkmar Hübschmann

The arrow has missed its target and has landed right in a puddle. Everyone can imagine how the arrow looks now.

What to do? Should one stick it back in the quiver in that condition or use it for the next shot?

Neither is a nice idea, and it is not at all necessary, as long as one has a tassel.

One holds the tassel with one hand; with the other, one pulls the arrow through it.

If the tassel gets very dirty after intensive use, one can simply wash it out in lukewarm water with some wool detergent and let it dry—now it is ready to be used again.

Making such a tassel is just as simple as using it.

The cardboard is cut as shown in the picture and a hole is punched in a bottom corner.

The end of the skein of yarn is passed through the hole and knotted. Then one wraps as much yarn as is wanted on the cardboard spool.

The upper edge of the wrapped yarn is now tied together with the leather belt.

After the knot is cut off, the lower edge of the wrapped yarn is cut with a knife. In the upper area, directly under the leather belt, one now binds the bundle of yarn together firmly (with twine).

Finally, the carbine hook is fastened to the leather belt, so that the tassel can be attached handily near the grip, for example, on the quiver.

Needed are:
• A skein of woolen yarn,
• A piece of cardboard (ca. 2 x 12 cm),
• Yarn (or art twine),
• A leather belt,
• A carbine hook, available from a shoemaker or saddler.

Bow-stringing Cord

Volkmar Hübschmann

Whoever would like to string his bow has various ways to do it.
Some of them, though, can damage the bow, for example, by twisting the limbs.
Others can injure the archer if his hand slips.
Stringing the bow with a cord is especially safe and comfortable.

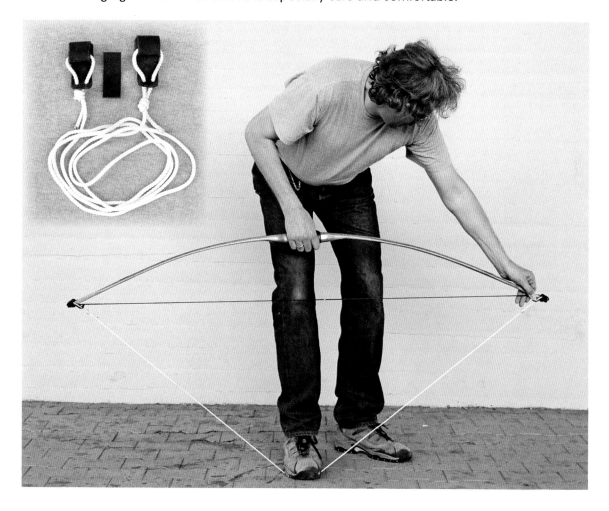

Stringing the bow

The bowstring must be in the notch of the lower limb, and the end cap is placed over the tip with the string.

The string loop is on the upper limb under the notch. The end cap is placed on the tip, but the notches must remain free.

Now one places his right foot on the middle of the stringing cord, takes the grip of the bow in his right hand and pulls the bow upward. The loop of the bowstring is pushed along the limb with the left hand until it slips into the notch.

Bow-stringing Cord

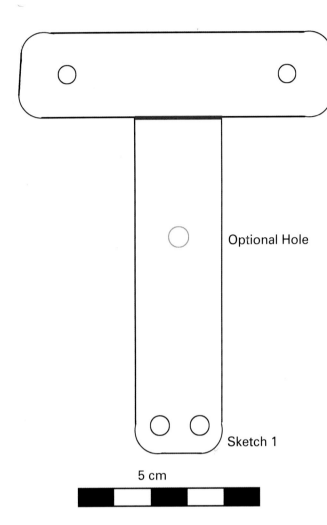

Optional Hole

Sketch 1

5 cm

A stringing cord is relatively easy to make. For it, one needs plaited nylon cord 4 mm thick (commercially available); 2.5 meters are enough for bows up to 70 inches long (1.78 meter).

For the end caps one needs sturdy leather some 2 to 3 mm thick, two hollow rivets and a punch of 4 mm diameter.

Two T-shaped pieces (Sketch 1) are cu out of the leather.

The end caps must fit the tips of the bow that is to be strung.

The pattern shown here is more or less a universal model.

It is best to make the leather caps first of heavy paper or cardboard and place them on the tips for testing.

If the caps do not fit, the pattern has to be adjusted to fit.

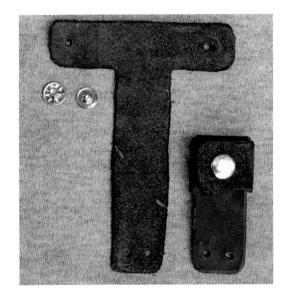

When one has cut two T-shaped leather pieces and punched the holes for the rivets with a punch or punching pliers, the leather is folded.

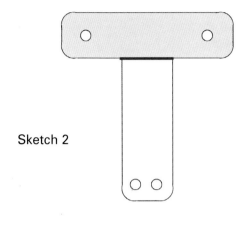

Sketch 2

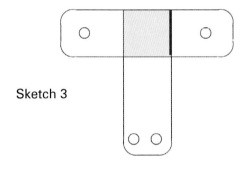

Sketch 3

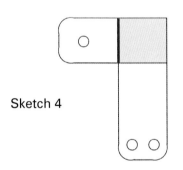

Sketch 4

Step 1
The horizontal piece of the T is folded forward at the red line (Sketch 1).

Step 2
Now fold the horizontal piece of the T forward a second time (Sketch 2).

Step 3
The right side of the T is folded backward on the red line (Sketch 3).

Step 4
Then the left side of the T is folded backward along the red line (Sketch 4).

Step 5
The two holes in the left and right sides of the horizontal piece must now lie one over the other. The hollow rivet is stuck through these two holes. Whoever wants to can also put the rivet through the optional hole in the vertical part of the T. Finally, one hammers the two pieces of the hollow rivet together with a hammer (placing a strip of metal under it).

Step 6
The second end cap is made in the same way as described in steps 1-5.

Step 7
As shown in the pictures, one now runs the nylon cord through the holes and the loop above the "pocket".

Step 8
Now the string has to be shortened to the required length and knotted.

If the upper end cap should slide too far over the tip and cover the notches, one can cure this by putting a piece of leather in U form in the "pocket" of the upper end cap.

Quivers

Thoughts about quivers

Tooled back quivers

Back quivers with built-in knife sheath

St. Charles quivers

Oetzi quivers made of felt

Hip quivers in Plains Indian style

Tooled hip quivers

Holster quivers

Other quiver types

Thoughts About Quivers

Volkmar Hübschmann

The simplest way to transport arrows is probably by sticking them into one's belt or back trouser pocket, or simply carrying a few arrows in one's hand along with the bow.
In the long run, though, these are not satisfactory solutions.
A good quiver is an extremely useful utensil, as it protects the arrows and holds them ready to be taken out. But what kind of quiver is the right one, and for whom?

The first question that one should ask is: Where and for what type of archery is the quiver to be used?

An archer who is only shooting at targets in a flat field surely has different requirements in a quiver than an archer who is fighting his way through rough country in a 3-D tournament, similarly to a bow hunter. I would rather not go into the aspects of safe and soundless transportation of hunting arrows with hunting points here.

For many traditional archers, the back quiver is the "traditional quiver", period. Like every quiver, the back quiver also has its advantages, for it is no hindrance when one is walking. The disadvantage, though, is that, depending on how it is built, it and the arrows get caught in branches more or less often.

Hip and belt quivers allow one to see the arrows without dislocating his neck. Some archers also find pulling out arrows more pleasant than from a back quiver, and a not-to-be-undervalued argument for the hip quiver in Saxton Pope style is that the arrows stay dry longer in the rain when carried under a poncho.
The disadvantage of this type of quiver is that it can be a disturbance when walking and often gets in the way of one's knees when shooting.

I think the best quiver is the one that the archer gets along with best—a very individual matter, and partially also a question of style. An Indian hip quiver just does not go with an English longbow. No limits are placed on one's imagination when making a quiver, either in form or the choice of materials. It is only important that the quiver fulfills its purpose.

The following building directions thus do not need to be followed exactly, but only offer a certain basic scheme of things. All quivers must naturally be fitted to the arrow length and the stature of the archer. The measurements in the instructions are based on 28-inch arrows, unless something else is noted.

Beginners are inclined to make a gigantic quiver to be able to carry a goodly number of arrows. In practice, a quiver with a capacity of 12 to, at most, 15 arrows has proved to be fully satisfactory. Larger quivers only make sense when one would also like to carry the two halves of a take-down bow.

Since most archers do not stick with one bow over the course of time, there is also no reason not to build several quivers oneself, based on considerations of terrain, weather, and the style of one's bow or clothing, etc.

I hope that with the following instructions everyone gets enough information and inspiration to build his dream quiver (or several) himself.

Tooled Back Quivers

Lederarbeiten: Joey Frosch, Text und Fotos: Volkmar Hübschmann

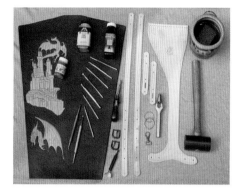

Leatherwork: Joey Frosch; text and photos: Volkmar Hübschmann

The first step should be the making of a cardboard pattern. Changes can be made to it, or a new pattern made, until the cardboard quiver completely suits one's own conceptions.

Beginning by cutting the leather is not a good idea. It would be a waste of good leather, for once you have cut it wrong, it is usually useless for the project. And it does no harm to develop a certain respect when you use the material, for after all, an animal gave its life to provide the leather.

When all the leather parts are cut and the edges prepared, tooling can begin.
The motif of this quiver (already finished) was applied to the leather with a *plastic template* (a heavy plastic foil on which the motif is applied in relief form). For this, the leather is moistened and the pattern of the *plastic template* is pressed into the leather with the spoon side of a *modeling tool*.

After tooling the motif is finished, the whole rest of the surface is likewise structured with a tooling iron, and the holes for the thorns of the buckles, plus the rivet holes, are punched.

Now the tooled surfaces cam be shadowed with rubbed-on finish (*antique leather stain*), which is applied with a sponge. The background is colored with leather paint (*Leather-Dye* or acrylic paint) that is applied with a brush.

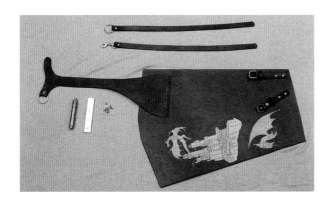

After painting, the buckles (don't forget the connections for the ends of the belts!), the brass rings and carbine hooks are riveted on.

The small belts at the bottom are riveted to the quiver or screwed on with *Chicago screws*; the shoulder strap is sewn on.

At intervals of some 7 mm, the holes for the plaited edge are cut all around the quiver. Now it is possible to sew the quiver together provisionally with sewing thread and determine the shape of the bottom.

When the bottom is cut, this is likewise structured, painted and pierced. Be sure that the number of holes and their intervals match those opposite them, so there will be no problem in binding them.

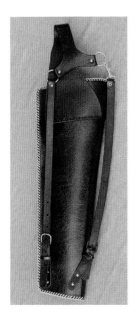

The last major step is the laborious and time-consuming plaiting together of the quiver. Whoever would like to can also sew small pieces of bone (hair pipe) into the opening of the quiver as arrow dividers.

Finally, the length of the shoulder strap must be adjusted to fit the stature of the archer.

Back Quiver with Integrated Knife Sheath

Volkmar Hübschmann

This back quiver is made for my arrow length (28.5 inches). It measures 66 cm long, which is relatively long, meaning that part of the feathering is inside the quiver.

By my experience, back quivers with just one strap are somewhat problematic. The weight of the arrows makes them slide, and one is constantly busy correcting the position of the quiver. This problem is normally solved by using two straps and a three-point fastening on the chest.

But there is another possible way to prevent sliding—attach a knife sheath with a large and correspondingly heavy knife directly to the shoulder strap.

The weight of the knife forms a counterweight to the arrows, and the quiver does not slide any more.

I can ignore the feeling that the knife could get in the way while shooting.

A general disadvantage of back quivers is that the arrows that project some distance out at the top can catch on things.
This problem can be solved to some extent by sewing the shoulder strap not directly to the bottom end of the quiver, but rather some 10 cm farther up. Using this trick makes the quiver hang somewhat lower, and the arrows get caught much less often.
In direct comparison, the difference is clear to see.

Back Quiver with Integrated Knife Sheath

Necessary Tools and Materials:
- Steel ruler
- Varnish knife or Opinel
- Art twine
- Various leather needles
- Plastic hammer
- Two different awls
- Wooden block (working surface)
- Hammer
- Brass rivets
- Punches of different diameters
- Punching pliers
- Edge breaker
- Various needles
- Stitch sinker
- Dividers
- Flat pliers
- Leather shears

All coverings were done with contact cement (Bostik N 726).

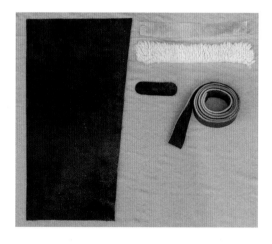

1. A piece of leather is cu in a trapezoidal shape. Here it necessary to make a cardboard pattern first. It is important that the edge of the quiver opening and the lower edge, to which the bottom is attached, are straight.

2. When the leather for the quiver is cut, a strip of rawhide 5 cm wide and an equally wide strip of lamb hide can be cut.

3. By sticking the cardboard pattern for the quiver together with tape and standing the resulting tube on a cardboard box, the shape of the base can be drawn.

Cut out the form and transform the outline to the leather. Then cut out the bottom.

4. Now leather straps 4.5 cm wide are cut. For the long strip I needed some 95 cm, for the short lower strap, onto which the buckle is sewn, some 18 cm.

Be sure always to remember that it makes a lot of difference whether one will be shooting in a T-shirt or in thick winter clothing!

5. The strip of lamb hide is now stuck to the rawhide. The two strips glued together are then stuck exactly on the upper rim (inside!) of the quiver. The rawhide stiffens the quiver rim; the lamb's wool protects the feathering.

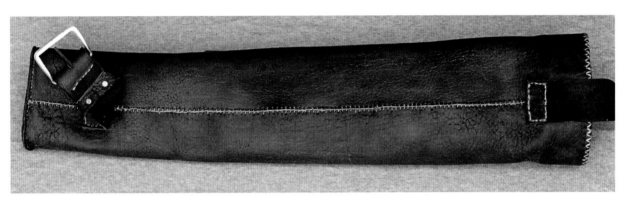

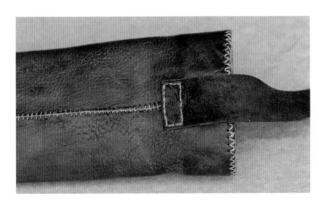

6. The two vertical edges are now pre-pierced (making the holes with the awl in advance makes the sewing much easier), and the quiver is sewn together into a tube.

Note: Be sure to attach the leather about every 5 centimeters. Flower thread has worked best for me, for the leather must not be displaced during sewing.
The seam must match, hole to hole, as it would otherwise have to be separated and sewn anew. I would like to spare the reader this frustrating experience.

7. The upper belt is sewn on below the edging.

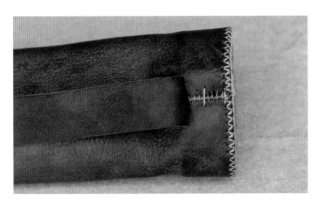

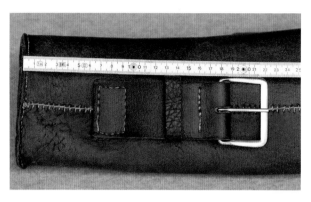

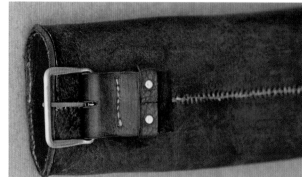

8. On the lower strap, the belt buckle and the loop for the upper end of the belt are riveted. It does not hurt to glue the belt at the places where it is sewn.

9. After the strap is fastened to the quiver, the bottom is sewn on. Here too, be sure to attach the bottom with flower thread o avoid the leather being displaced.

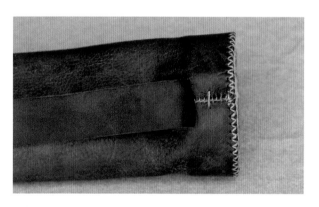

10. To strengthen the bottom, one can glue a thick piece of chamois-tanned deer leather or rubber onto the bottom from inside.

11. Two and a half centimeters from the rim of the quiver, to the left and right near the seam, make one hole each in the quiver with the awl and pull a small leather belt through these holes.

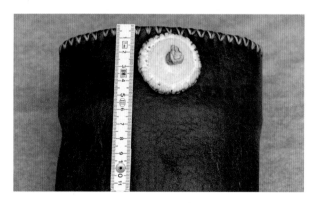

Directly opposite the seam, make a somewhat larger hole in the quiver and pull the two twisted ends of the leather strap through it.

For decoration, I use an antler rose drilled through the middle. The ends of the strip are pulled through it and knotted. The leather strip pulls the quiver opening into an oval shape and also serves as an arrow separator.

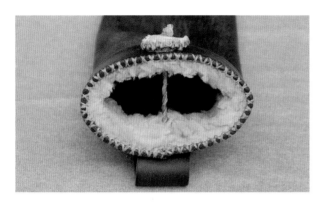

12. A decorative border around the rim of the quiver adds a neat closing.

13. The quiver is now ready to hold arrows. With a filled quiver on one's back, the narrowest and widest holes for the buckle provide for wearing a T-shirt or heavy winter clothes. The space between these holes can be holed to meet one's needs.

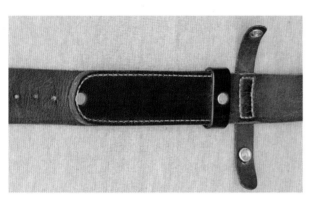

14. The quiver is now practically finished; now comes the knife sheath. It consists of two layers of hard leather glued together. The precise directions for making the sheath are found in the "Archers' Knives" chapter.

15. A little above the first hole in the shoulder strap, the knife sheath is first glued on, then sewn and also riveted at the corners. To reinforce the blade opening, a leather strip is riveted to the front and back and glued (on the front).

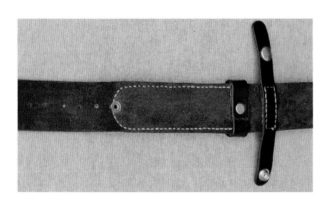

16. Above the blade, a securing strap with a snap button is sewn and glued to the back of the strap.

To rivet the snap button, one needs a special tool; here the friendly shoemaker or saddler can help again (on the back).

17. The knife sheath is painted with leather paint to match the quiver.

18. To make the quiver weathertight and protect the leather, it is rubbed completely with leather grease. This treatment, regularly repeated, guarantees a long happy life to leather goods.

St. Charles Quiver

Uwe Gangnus

A problem of typical quivers—also in our latitudes—at least in rainy summers—is that the feathering gets wet.

One way of keeping the feathering dry, even under bad weather conditions (besides the "Oetzi style" quiver) is by using a quiver of the type that the legendary American archer Glenn St. Charles developed at the end of the 1950s and early 1960s and the "Bear Archery" firm sold until 1974.

The basic building principle of this quiver is fixing the arrows in a rigid frame, consisting of firm bottom and cover and a linking piece to which the carrying system is attached.

The bottom is open on both sides, the arrows being held fast with point and notch between the bottom and top, for example, in a foam rubber cushion, The "feathering element" in this system is a piece of foam rubber, 3 cm thick, in the cover, and one cm of rubber at the bottom. The feathering is protected from the weather by a plastic or leather cap that is attached to the cover.

If one does not make the middle section adjustable as to length, as is done as a rule in its younger brother, the Cat quiver, the quiver must be planned exactly to the length of the arrows it will hold:

Arrow length
+ thickness of rubber bottom
+ thickness of foam top
- 1.5 cm
= open distance between top and bottom

Two variants of a carrying system can be considered.
One is the backpack type with two carrying straps. The advantage of this system is that the quiver stays very firmly in the middle of the back and does not swing while walking.
Its disadvantage: Putting the arrows back is rather difficult.

In the second type, one carries the quiver on one strap diagonally across the back, somewhat like a classical back quiver. Putting arrows back is thus simplified, but the quiver is not so stable on one's back.

In general, taking arrows out of this type of quiver can be done simply and without sound regardless of the type of carrying system, which explains its popularity, at least at times, among bow hunters.

On the other hand, putting arrows back is somewhat difficult, so that the St. Charles quiver can scarcely be regarded as the optimal type for training use, where many arrows have to be shot. It is more suitable as an alternative to the back quiver in rainy tournaments.

St. Charles Quiver

Materials

For the quiver frame, as much strapping or plaited leather cord as needed
- Watertight wood glue
- 6 wood screws, 3 x 40 mm
- Boat paint for painting and decorations as you wish

The measurements of the top and bottom can be varied much according to the quiver's planned capacity; the length of the central part, of course, always depends on the length of the arrows to be carried.

If one stays more or less within the suggested measurements:
- Top oval 145 x 100 mm,
- Bottom plate 80 x 100 mm,
- Bide connecting piece 75 or 45 mm,

The quiver will hold 12 to 14 arrows loosely, as long as plate or field points are used.

First the outlines of the top, bottom and connecting piece are transferred to the plywood.

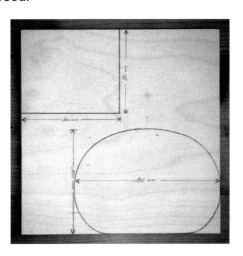

The individual pieces are cut out and all edges carefully smoothed.

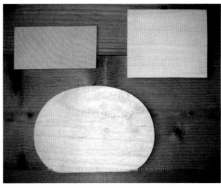

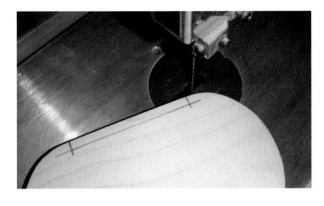

A cutout is made in the cover plate for the connecting part, so that later the upper cap can be placed on the quiver without a "dent".

The individual parts are now glued to each other and, for security, screwed together with three 3 x 40 mm screws each (using 2 mm bored holes).

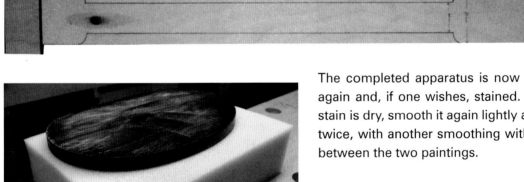

The completed apparatus is now sanded again and, if one wishes, stained. As soon as the stain is dry, smooth it again lightly and paint it at least twice, with another smoothing with K240 sandpaper between the two paintings.

After the paint has dried, the rubber is glued onto the bottom plate and the foam onto the cover. A spray adhesive from a can is especially good for this.

The extra spray material can be cut off even with the cover plate, using a sharp knife.

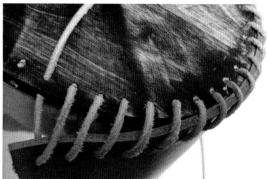

To be able to attach the leather cover, the top plate has holes bored in it angling to the outside. To make sure the holes are even, a pattern should be used.

The leather for the cover is cut to the outline of the top plate, holes are punched in it with punch pliers at the intervals of the bored holes, and then it is "sewn on" with leather straps 100 cm long, one from the left and one from the right.

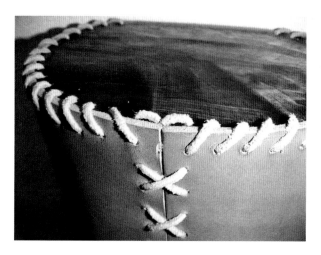

At the front of the cover, the two straps are pushed inside to close the front part of the cover.

After attaching the shoulder strap, the St. Charles quiver is finished.

Oetzi Quiver made of Felt

Andrea Gangnus

The idea of making a quiver of the type that Oetzi used came to us during a visit to a display on the glacier man.

The advantages of the Oetzi quiver are above all in the protection of the feathering, especially from moisture.
Unlike the original one made of chamois hide, felt seems like the ideal material to us, as it can be made with relatively little material and few tools. Besides, it repels water.

To make it, one needs, besides time, patience and strength, only unspun wool, soap, hot water, a laundry sprinkler, hand towels and a stencil.
Making such a quiver took me about six hours. Whoever has not yet used felt probably needs more time and should perhaps practice first on a smaller piece.
One can gain experience with a belt pouch to hold the utensils one needs in archery.
Best of luck!

Oetzi Quiver made of Felt

General information on the felt

General Information about Felting Characteristics

Felt is, among other things, water-repellent and not flammable. Its most important characteristic for a quiver is probably that it is watertight, to protect the feathering.

Felt, to be sure, is not stable in terms of shape and not very resistant to wear. As in the original Oetzi quiver, this quiver thus took on its stability of form from a wooden piece on the side.

The shoulder strap can be made of plaited leather. Felt has not worked well here.

Wool

Store-bought sheep's-wool fleece is especially good for felting, since the wool is combed flat and the needed thin layers can be worked out carefully.

Soap

Olive soap, which can be bought in a cake or as flakes, is very well suited for making felt. It is dissolved in hot water.

To ¼ liter of hot water, add 2 to 3 tablespoons of soap. Thus the solution becomes nicely smooth, so the fingers can glide over the wool better. The heat supports the felting process.

Felting Process

In felting, the wool, laid on a pattern in several thin layers, is sprinkled with hot soapy water. The wool should be wet, but not swimming. Now one runs one's flat hand over the wool in light circular movements. The wool must not be moved or stick to the hands.

A fine film forms on the surface. The wool turns to felt, the fine fibers link with each other. Again and again, the piece of felt is sprinkled with hot soapy water and felted further by added rubbing and ever-stronger pressure, until no individual wool fibers stand up any more.

Fulling

When the wool is felted to the point where a homogeneous piece has been formed, out of which no fibers can project any more, the fulling begins. The felt is rolled in a towel and rolled back and forth by hand on a smooth surface. The pressure is slowly increased. The felt thickens and shrinks. The raw felt is rolled alternately longitudinally and transversely. Since the shrinking always occurs in the direction of the rolling, the size of the finished piece can be influenced by the fulling direction. Depending on the wool, thickness and pressure, the felt shrinks about 30%.

Pattern

To produce a "hollow body", the front and back sides must be separated from each other in the fulling. All materials that are not felted in the process and whose edges can be felt clearly through the wool layers are suitable, such as thick cardboard, a piece of PVC floor material or air-bubble plastic.

The pattern has the shape of the object to be felted, but must be some 30% larger.

I like to use PVC.

Instructions for the Oetzi Quiver

Material

Approximately 350 grams of unspun sheep's-wool.

My pattern has the dimensions:

110 x 33 cm above or 24 cm below.
The later size of the quiver is painted on the pattern.

Wrapping

From the wool fleece, fine layers of wool are pulled off and wrapped firmly and evenly around the pattern in several layers.

One wraps once vertically and once horizontally. The more fine layers, the better the wool felts, and the more compact the felt becomes.

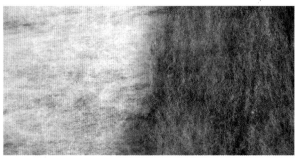

It is very important to wrap very evenly, since otherwise thin places or even holes can occur.

One should wrap the felt around the edges very carefully. If the whole thing is too loose, the top and bottom layers come into contact in felting, and thick bulges result in that location.

Four or five layers of wool should suffice to make a sufficiently thick felt. I have used light and dark brown wool alternately, so that the direction can be seen more clearly in the photos.

Since the wool fibers hook onto each other and the colors mix, my piece is a mixed light brown. In this way one can create one's own preferred color. The careful wrapping takes about an hour.

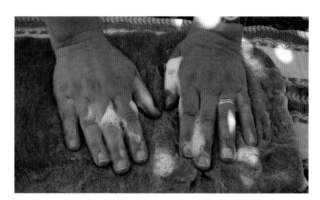

Felting

Some 3 to 4 tablespoons of olive soap are dissolved in ¼ liter of hot water. This mixture is soapy enough to let one's hands move lightly over the wool layers.

Now lay the piece of felt on a big towel that can absorb the moisture. With a small spray bottle, first moisten the edges, and then begin carefully to rub over the wool in small circular motions.

One must be careful that only the wool that one wants to felt gets wet. Always work just a small surface, for the hotter the damp wool is, the more easily it felts. Always press the wool against the pattern with the flats of the hands, so that the front and back sides do not come into contact with each other.

When a fine film is formed, one can always rub more firmly. But be careful! If the wool is pushed too hard, holes result.

When you have worked along the edges of the pattern, turn the piece and work the edges along the back.

In the middle of the quiver, the airy, dry layers of wool are still raised.

Only now is the middle worked just like the edges.

Spray piece by piece, stroke and rub with your flat hand.

Rubbing pushes out the air between the wool fibers, so that it looks as if the piece would be much too big. By further rubbing, the fibers become felted and shrink. Thus the wool tightens around the pattern. One must just be careful not to add any folds.

A possible problem is that not everything is well felted with each other and individual strands of wool hang loose. These can be pinched or cut off carefully. The place should be sprayed again with soapy water and worked carefully.

  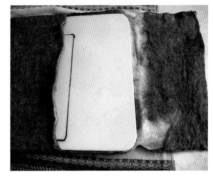

When the whole quiver is felted, cut the felt at the lower edge of the future flap, about 15 cm from the upper rim, and pull the pattern out.

To be able to open the flap, the two edges have to be cut 15 cm.

Now you can see whether the edges were worked out right, and whether there are bulges or holes.
Holes can be repaired by laying a piece of unspun wool on the spot and felting it dry with a felt needle.
When the wool is firmly worked in, work the spot again with soapy water.

Small holes or thin places will thicken through the shrinking process during fulling.

Finally, the entire piece is well rinsed under running water. There must not be any more soap in it. The olive soap would turn yellow in time, and the quiver would have ugly blotches.

Now it just needs to dry, which takes one or two days. Since felt can be shaped when wet, and then keeps that shape, one should now get the quiver into shape. I have rounded the edges slightly, likewise the bottom. One either stuffs it with a towel or paper, or lays it in the right position.

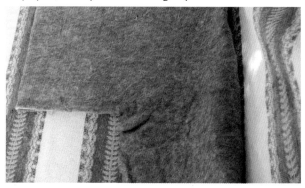

Fulling

When the felt is firm enough, it is fulled. Thereby it takes on stability and its correct size. The quiver is wrapped in a dry towel and the roll is rolled back and forth, lightly at first, then with steadily increasing pressure.

Now unwrap the piece and turn it over. Wrap and roll it again. The felt piece must be wrapped in all directions, both front and back, always longitudinally and transversely. In addition, the piece must be turned so that the edges lie one on the other and turn the quiver so that the inside comes out.

The felt now shrinks increasingly, and the surface becomes slightly bumpy. This is proof that the wool fibers are hooked firmly to each other.
This process takes at least an hour and is very demanding. Whoever has less strength in his arms can lay the roll on the floor and roll it with his feet.

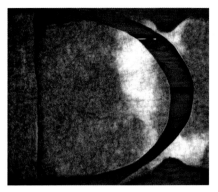  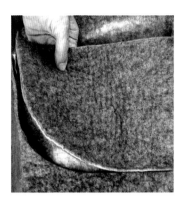

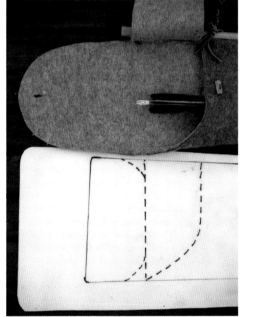

Preparation

After drying, cut the upper flap half-round with sharp shears and the side flap quarter-round.
If the quiver turns out to be too long for your own arrows, simply do not cut the flaps on the upper edge, but appropriately farther down.

One can see the arrangement and function of the flaps in this picture. Since the shrinking process depends on the thickness of the wool layers and the pressure during fulling, the exact size cannot be predicted accurately.

A hazel branch the length of the quiver is bored through a number of times and tied to the side of the quiver.

The felt can easily be pierced with a needle. A leather needle with a sharp point is also helpful.
A plaited leather cord is also fastened to the staff and quiver as a carrier belt.

Now sew one button on the front and one on the back. Cut a buttonhole lengthwise in the felt, so it will not bulge out.

The Oetzi-type felt quiver is finished.
The finished quiver holds 12 to 14 arrows 29 inches long.

Hip Quiver in Plains Indian Style

Leatherwork: Joey Frosch; text and photos: Volkmar Hübschmann

For this quiver one needs a complete hide of chamois-tanned deer leather (about 1.2 square meters). Whether one decides in favor of leather polished on both sides, or for so-called grained leather, is a matter of taste.

The polished leather takes the paint better, the unpolished grained leather is more stable and water- and dirt-repellent.

The deer leather absolutely must be lined; unlined, it would contract too much in time, especially the shoulder strap.

All strong fabrics that do not fray too much are suitable for linings, as is thin rawhide. The latter, though, is not as suitable for lining the shoulder strap. The quiver described here was lined with thin woolen cloth.

Dimensions of the depicted quiver:
• Length 55 cm
• Width 17 cm
• Carrying length 62 cm

The length of the shoulder strap naturally depends on the archer's stature and on what height the quiver is to be carried at. One can start with a length of 1.6 to 1.8 meters.

Since it it problematic to cut a strap of this length from a single piece, it is practical to make the strap of two or three equally long pieces.

Required Materials and Tools

• 1 complete hide of deer leather (ca. 1.2 square meters)
about 1.5 lfm of lining material
• Contact cement
• Glass beads, decorative nails, plastic cord
• Earth paint, leather paint (saddle paint) for fixing, imitation eagle feathers, horsehair, sheet-metal cones
• Hardwood rod, about finger-thick, somewhat longer than the quiver
• Leather shears, cutting knife
• Zigzag shears
• Leather needles
• Awl

All gluing was done with Bostik N 726 contact cement.

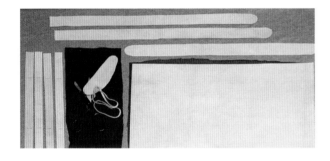

1. Cut the rectangular piece of leather for the quiver, the three pieces for the shoulder strap (about 4 to 4.5 cm wide), and the four holding strips (about 30 x 3.5 cm).

2. One can make leather straps out of rounded scraps of leather by cutting them in spiral form with shears, always at the same width.

3. Glue the lining to the rectangular piece of leather. At the front, at the subsequent quiver opening, leave a strip about 4 cm wide free.

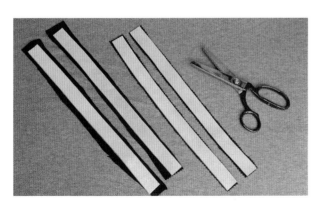

4. Glue the lining onto the three strips for the shoulder strap and the four holding strips. The holding strips should be glued only to 10 to 12 cm from the ends. Leave the lining 1 to 2 cm longer and wider on the unglued ends. Cut the edges at these longer and wider places with the zigzag shears.
Cut all other edges even with the leather.

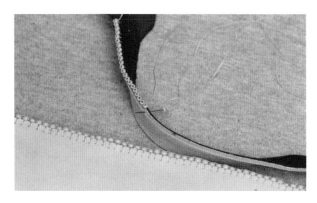

5. Decorate all the edges with beads (see sketch), which will hinder twisting of the soft deer leather.

6. Apply glue to the unlined strips on the quiver opening and attach them. The resulting bulge adds strength and will later be decorated with beads.

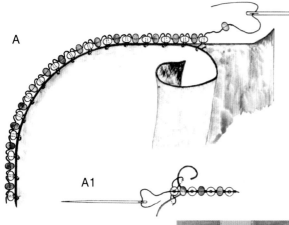

A

A1

7. Fold the quiver in the middle and sew the seam (parallel to the quiver rod) together. Here too, the edge decoration is used and the seam decorated with beads.

About the sketch:
The side view (A) and the view (A1) show a possible way to link between cloth and leather.

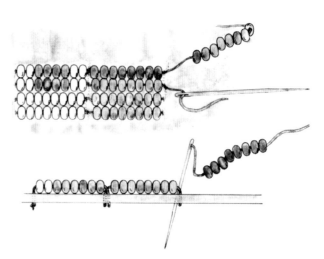

8. Surround the quiver opening with beads.

9. Position the holding strips, also adorned with beads (edge stitching), glue them on and sew them fast.

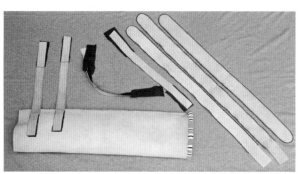

10. Cut the ends of the holding straps that are not glued to the lining into fringe.

11. Tie the quiver bottom together with self-cut leather strips and let them hang down as long fringe.
Note: Only make the holes that the leather strips are to pas through with the awl.
Never punch leather with the punch pliers, for the holes will grow wider.

12. Slide the quiver rod (seal the wood with linseed oil) through the holding straps and fasten it with decorative nails.

13. Tie the three parts of the shoulder strap together with leather strips.

14. The quiver is now finished to the point that the suitable positions for the shoulder strap on the quiver rod can be determined. Sew the ends of the shoulder strap and, if you choose, also fasten them with decorative nails.

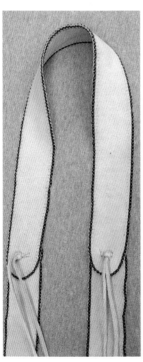

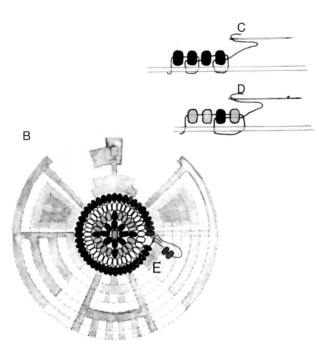

15. Making bead rosettes on a round piece of leather is shown in the sketch.

Making the rosettes
- Draw the desired motif (dotted lines in drawing B).
- Sew on central beads and first row, as in drawing C.
- Sew on following rows of beads as in drawing D.
- Finally, as in drawing E, draw the thread through the whole row, to make the beads lie evenly.

16. The quill of the imitation eagle feather is cut back to half of its thickness to about 4 cm.

The end of the quill remains unworked. A few drops of glue are put in the resulting groove.

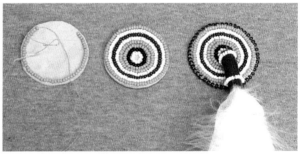

17. The end of the quill is bent backward and stuck into the groove.

Thus a loop is made, by which the feather is attached.

Under the loop, a strip of lining material is wrapped around the quill and glued.

A wrapping decorated with beads provides a decorative closing.

18. With a metal cone, a bundle of horsehair is enclosed and is sewn to the middle of a bead rosette.

19. The back of the rosette is painted with glue; then it is glued and sewn to the quiver.

The designs for the beadwork were taken from: *Indianische Perlenarbeiten—Das deutsche Beadwork-Handbuch—Geschichte—Materialien—Techniken,* by Peter Haug. Printed with kind permission of Dietmar Kuegler, Verlag für Amerikanistik.

Tooled Hip Quiver

Leatherwork: Joey Frosch; Text and photos: Volkmar Hübschmann

The quiver has the following dimensions: Length 56 cm, width 18 cm.

The attachment for the belt is 8 cm high on the side leading to the quiver opening. On the side leading to the bottom it is 26.5 cm high and has a width of 10 cm.

For all gluing work, a contact cement *(Bostik N 726)* was used.

1. Cut a rectangular piece of leather and break the edges.

2. Transfer the motif.

3. Carry out the tooling work and structure the background.

4. Paint the tooling work with acrylic leather paint.

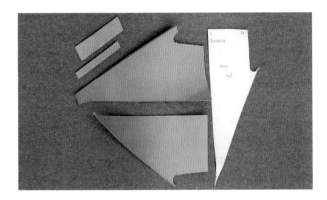

5. Cut the four individual pieces for the belt hanger (here too, a cardboard pattern is recommended) and break the edges.

Glue the two leather strips that form the "canal" for the belt to the back of the hanger parallel, about 5 cm apart.

6. Angle the lower edge of the bottom strip (a *Super Skiver* is used, which creates a smooth transition from the belt hanger to the actual quiver.

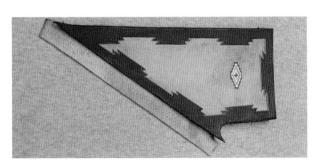

7. Glue the tooled and painted front to the back of the belt hanger.

8. Glue the belt hanger with the projecting strip to the inside of the quiver.

9. Pierce all the edges and the transition from the hanger to the quiver for the plaited band.
The places at which the belt passes through the hanger are not plaited.

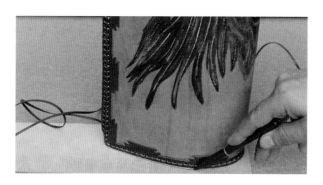

10. When the quiver is plaited to this extent, it is placed on a piece of leather and the bottom is traced.

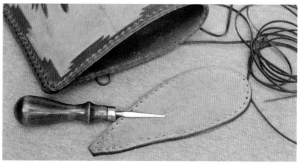

11. Cut out the bottom, structure and pierce it.

12. Attach the bottom.

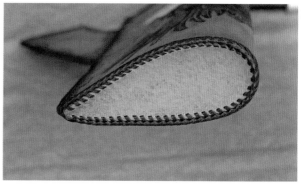

13. Treat the finished quiver with leather paint.

Holster Quiver

Stefan Schwed

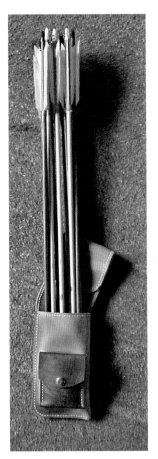
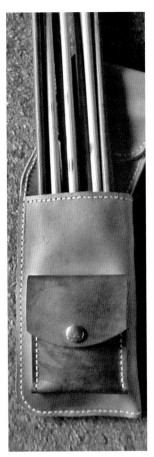

A simple holster quiver for the belt

1. Making a pattern.

I use thin cardboard, which can be worked simply and yet offers better stability than paper. The dimensions, of course, are yours to set. Here is an example:

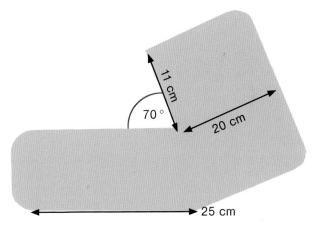

11 cm
70°
20 cm
25 cm

2. Transfer to the leather.

First one must decide whether the quiver is to be worn on the left or right side and lay out the pattern appropriately.

When transferring to the leather, I recommend that you use a pencil, since ball-point pen markings can be removed from the leather only with difficulty if one makes a mistake.

Whoever would like to harden the quiver later, as described under #9, should not use colored or painted leather, but only plain leather.

3. Cutting out

For cutting, I use special leather shears, but one can, of course, also use a carpet knife or something similar.

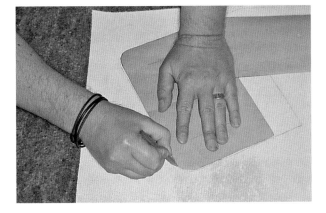

Holster Quiver

4. Ripping the holes

Ripping the holes for later sewing together is best done with a compass; I use a drawing compass.

Here the space between holes and the distance from the edge are both 5 mm.

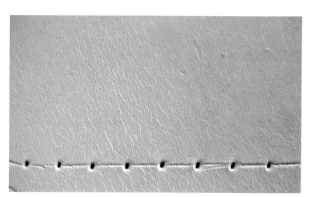

5. Punching or boring holes

To make the numerous holes, one can use either a sewing awl or a leather-sewing machine.
I prefer a small hand boring machine with a 1.5-mm borer; this always works fastest.

6. Making a thread groove

So that the thread does not get worn, use the seam sinker to cut a groove from hole to hole.

7. Sewing the pocket

The previously cut-out pocket must now be sewn on the front side. To close it, I use a simple press snap.

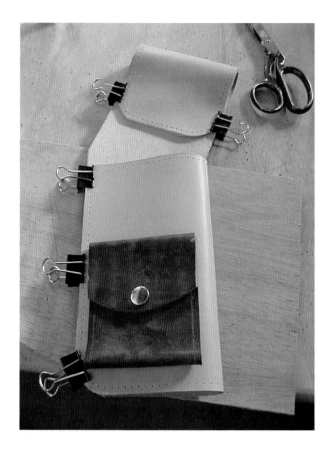

8. Sewing the holster together
For sewing, it is best to use waxed saddlers' thread. Synthetic saddlers' thread or art twine can be welded with a cigarette lighter.
Linen yarn can only be knotted and the thread end secured.

9. Applying patina to the holster
In principle, one is finished now, but the leather still needs treatment for protection and stability. I also like the leather to have or at least appear to have some patina.

For this, I use the following method:
First the entire holster is soaked at least half an hour. Before drying, it should be brought into the desired shape. It is best to stuff it with newspaper.
Then put it in an oven for about an hour at approximately 80 degrees C. The relatively quick drying has the advantage of making the leather very stiff and hard and also giving it a brownish color.
Whoever does not want to harden his holster quiver with heat can alternatively soak the quiver in lukewarm soda water (2 heaping tablespoons) for about a quarter hour.
After drying, the soda makes the leather hard.

10. Greasing or waxing the holster
For the finish, one should rub the holster with leather grease or leather wax. After everything is dry, the quiver can be put into use.

Other Quiver Types

Volkmar Hübschmann

The four illustrated quivers are regarded as inspirational. Perhaps someone will find a detail that he or she would like to adopt in making his or her own quiver.

All quivers are made for arrows that measure 28 ½ inches (72.4 cm) long.

Back quiver made of horsehide

This back quiver made of horsehide has a turned-back flap with fringe and a shoulder strap of grained deer leather. The shoulder strap is lined with red cloth. The length of the outer rim is 54 cm, that of the inner ring 50 cm. The quiver is 18 cm wide above, 14 cm below.

The shoulder strap is adjustable on a double-ring fastening.

The third strap is hooked to the rings with a carbine hook (3-point system).

The deer-leather fringes were wetted and strongly twisted; after drying, they remained in the twisted form.

The quiver is decorated with imitation grizzly claws and red glass beads with white insides, set into the hide.

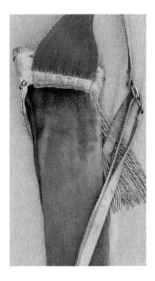

Through the bored antler discs there runs a knotted leather strap that serves as an arrow separator.

The front of the shoulder strap has an obsidian arrowhead sewn onto it.

Hip quiver made of horsehide, with mane

The quiver is 58 cm long and 19 cm wide. It is decorated with white and green glass beads (pony beads), and with feathers mounted in red felt cloth.

The quiver opening is rimmed with grained deer leather. The quiver rod is made of locust wood.

The shoulder strap consists of plaited strips of deer leather.

Belt quiver in Saxton Pope style

The quiver was sewn of beef leather, such as is also used for tooling. The quiver opening is strengthened with a flap of grained deer leather that also folds inward. The quiver is 57 cm long, the opening has a diameter of 11 cm, the round bottom 8.5 cm.

With the leather straps, which also serve as arrow dividers, a polished antler rose was attached.
For decoration, two metal beads are tied onto the ends of the leather strap.
The quiver is fastened with a sewn-on belt loop.

Quiver bottom.

Beef-leather back quiver, especially for transporting a take-down bow.

The outer rim of the quiver has a length of 57 cm, the inner rim of 51 cm. The flat back part is 20 cm wide above, 15 cm below. On this flat back part, two tubes open at the bottom (in principle, two very wide loops) of polished deer leather are sewn.

These tubes hold the two halves of the bow. The quiver flap is made of velour leather.

On the front and back of the flap are two antler buttons each, tied on (as arrow separators) with leather straps.
A cover of waxed canvas can be buttoned on by means of these buttons.

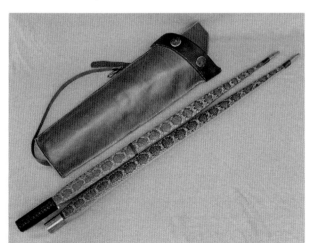

The stable canvas was impregnated with beeswax.
This cover protects the projecting limbs of the bow and the feathering of the arrows not only from rain, but during transport in general, such as on a motorcycle.

Arrow Shafts

Preliminary information

The self-notch

Spine-tester

Arrow-repair splices

Tapering of shafts

Tapering in practice

Making arrow shafts

Arrow straighteners

Shaft working

Painting arrows with Lego

Cresting

Wrapping arrows

Leather broadheads

Preliminary information

Volkmar Hübschmann

Before one begins to make arrows, one takes a close look at the straight shaft. How does the grain run?

If it is straight, the annual rings are visible as parallel lines to the outer rim. In the best case, the grain runs parallel throughout the whole length of the shaft.

Usually, though, it runs out of the shaft at one or more points, unfortunately. At these points the wood is much less sturdy than at places where the grain runs parallel.

Such places are "future breaking points": If the shaft breaks, as a rule it breaks there.

Tip   Notch

If one looks at the top of the shaft, one recognizes the grain emerging by the "flames".

The point of the emerging grain should always point upward, so that in case a shaft breaks at the moment of shooting, the broken arrow flies away upward, and not downward toward the bow hand.

Note: Go by the position of the leading feather!

The red line indicates the angle of the point that is in danger of breaking. The point points upward, away from the shooter's bow hand.

If a shaft shows such a course of grain in the middle area, it should be sorted out for reasons of safety!

Color makes the grain clear

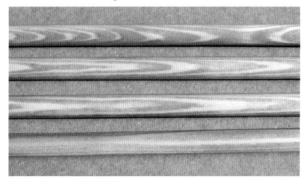

bad

medium

good

very good

Industrially made shafts are milled out of wooden boards. In this process, little or no attention can be given to the running of the grain. In shafts that are made of split wood, this problem does not exist, for the split follows the course of the grain.

Likewise, one need not worry about shafts made of shoots or bamboo.

Shafts made of glued wood lessen the problem of emerging grain. But every shaft that cannot be mass-produced industrially in the shortest time is either a case for the "do-it-yourselfer" or, if it is up for sale at all, correspondingly expensive.

After this brief excursion, back to industrially produced shafts.

If one, when looking closely at shafts, finds places where the grain emerges from the shaft, or other blemishes like small branches, remains of resin, etc., one notices these places. If the shaft must still be shortened to the individually required length, it may be possible to shorten it so that the bad spots are eliminated.

An arrow is most likely to break directly behind the head or in the front third of the shaft. Thus the "better end" of a shaft should always be forward.

Sometimes it is clear on which end the feathering and notch will be placed; sometimes it does not matter. If the grain runs out of the shaft at both ends, one puts that end forward in which the grain emerges less abruptly. Or in other words, the more pointed the angle at which the grain comes out, the more stable the shaft is at that point.

All this may sound complicated, but it is not. With some practice, one soon is able to judge his shafts correctly and, above all, make the right choice when buying shafts.

It is of course a prerequisite that the shafts have the right spine value and only minimal weight differences from each other.

The surfaces of wooden shafts must be sealed to prevent the wood from absorbing moisture (swelling, warping), and to heighten the mechanical strength of the surface.

For this purpose, resin oil and parquet wax, as well as colorless paint (boat paint) and glazes, are suitable.

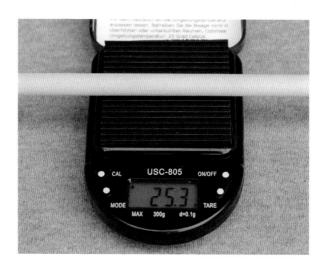

The Self-Notch

Volkmar Hübschmann

A self-notch is nothing but a slit cut into the shaft to take the bowstring. This slit must be sawed in the middle of the shaft and should always have the same depth in a set of arrows (about 8 mm).

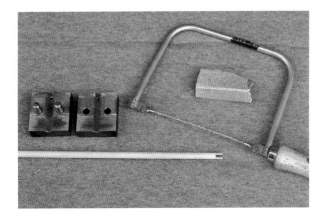

To saw my self-notches I use a special setup. I would like to describe the creation of a self-notch using this apparatus.

The advantage of this apparatus is that one can saw his notches quickly and precisely. Whether one absolutely needs such an apparatus must be decided by every individual.

Whoever has skill using tools and fingertip feeling can certainly do the job without it.

The shaft is inserted into the guiding channel of the two halves of the block, with the annual rings running parallel to the saw slit.
The shaft end ends even with the top of the block. The block with the shaft is then put into a vise.

With about a 3 mm wood drill, the shaft is drilled through from the guiding hole on the front of the block.

The vise is opened slightly and the shaft turned 90 degrees. The shaft is then screwed tight in this position. The saw slit still runs at a right angle to the annual rings.

With a round-bladed coping saw, the notch slit is cut in the middle. When sawing, one notices at once when the saw blade reaches the drilled hole.

The notch is sanded with fine sandpaper. No sharp angles may remain after sanding. The bottom of the notch must be rounded. By drilling a hole through the shaft, the bottom of the notch is made exactly half-round, and the slits are all of the same depth.

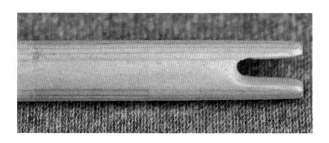

After the shaft has been given its final water-resistant treatment, a wrapping directly under the bottom of the notch protects the shaft from splitting.
The wrapping technique is the same one that is used to secure the feathering.

Spine-Tester

Michael Prinz

The reason for deciding to build a spine-tester was that some of my arrows did not fly as they really should have. My first thought was to buy myself a spine-tester, but the relatively high price put me off.

In Hilary Greenland's book (*Praktisches Handbuch fuer traditionelle Bogenschuetzen*) the principle of building a spine-tester is depicted, and I thought, why not build myself one?
The first attempt, though, failed, because it was not possible for me to turn the bending of the arrow into a spine value on the bending scale.

In the specialist literature I found the following advice:

> *"A shaft with a bend of 0.52 inches (13.2 mm) when weighted with a weight of 2 pounds (907 grams) represents a spine-value of 50 pounds."*

13.2 mm x 50 = 660 mm, or 26 inches, and distance between the two supporting points. With the thus derived formula:

$$\frac{660.4 \text{ mm (distance between supports)}}{X \text{ mm (bending)}} = \text{Spine value in pounds}$$

I could calculate any spine value by adding the bending of the shaft in mm as X.

With these values it is possible to calculate other spine values as well, and for the following reason: Shafts with equal diameters can have different spine values; the means of measuring in a spine-tester, though, is always the same.
The distance between the supporting points for the shaft, plus the testing weight and the shaft diameter, are always the same. The only difference is in the shaft.

Through different graining, number of annual rings, etc., shafts of the same diameter can be softer or stiffer, which means that the ratio of bending in mm to the spine-value is linear.

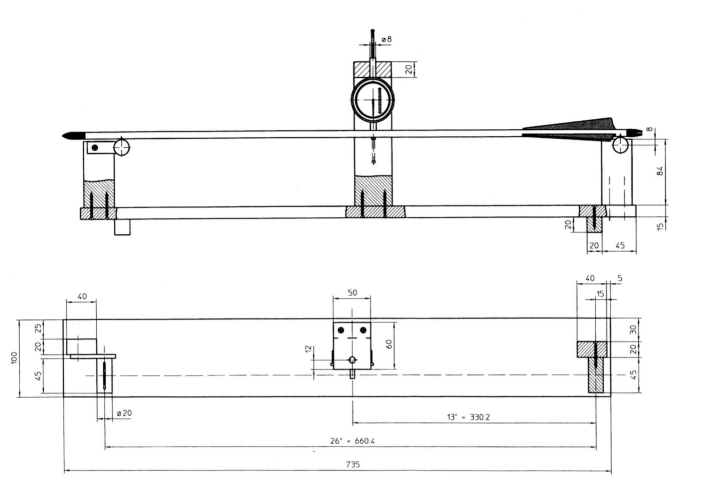

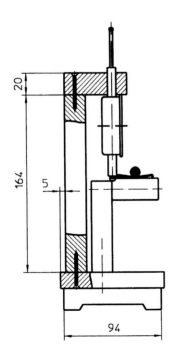

To be able to measure the bending, I have built the following spine-tester. It has no scale, but rather a measuring dial, such as are normally used in metalworking to measure plan and circular tolerances.

The great measured extent of 0 to 30 mm allows me to be able to measure spine-values from 22 pounds. By using a table, the measured millimeters can be read as spine-values.

The material that I used for the basic structure was ordinary wood.

Metal covering

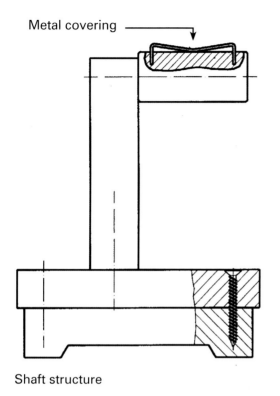

Shaft structure

The placement points of the shaft are made of round wood, but the first measuring attempts showed that the shafts do not slide well on the wooden frame and falsify the measuring results.
Therefore I have equipped the round material with an additional wire.

It is recommended that one of the placement points be made highly variable, so that the zero point can be set on the dial, if this cannot be zeroed directly by turning the scale.

Measuring dial

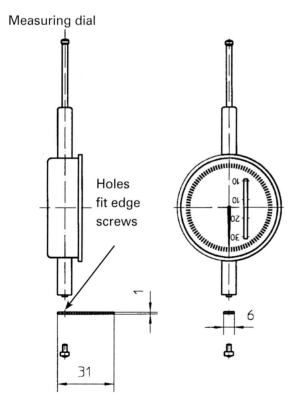

Holes fit edge screws

In the picture it can be seen that the dial is mounted on its head. Normally the dial is activated by pressure on the long measurement feeler, but in this case a thin metal strip is fastened on he opposite short side of the feeler, which forms the placement point for the shaft.

Measuring dial Type HK-Precision Measuring Dial ORION 33032
See source in Appendix.

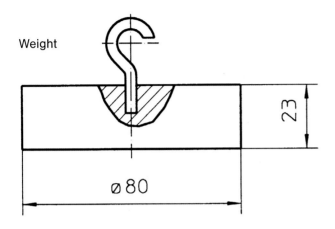

Weight

⌀ 80

23

By hanging the weight onto the shaft, the feeler is drawn out and the dial activated.

The hook is made by bending a wire 4 mm thick and glued into the weight with a two-component adhesive.

Before the weight is finished, the individual parts should be weighed again and corrected if necessary.

Weight with a screwed-on double brass hook.

The holes served to remove material, in order to set the weight (907 grams).

The rest of the procedure in building the spine-tester presumably need not be described in greater detail and can be derived from the drawings.

The given height masses of the placement points as well as the attachment of the dial refer to the dial cited below. If other products are used, these figures may have to be corrected.

Spine-Value	Bending	Spine-Value	Bending	Spine-Value	Bending	Spine-Value	Bending
lb	mm	lb	mm	lb	mm	lb	mm
30	22,0	41	16,1	51	12,9	61	10,8
31	21,3	42	15,7	52	12,7	62	10,6
32	20,6	43	15,3	53	12,4	63	10,4
33	20,0	44	15,0	54	12,2	64	10,3
34	19,4	45	14,7	55	12,0	65	10,1
35	18,8	46	14,3	56	11,8	66	10,0
36	18,3	47	14,0	57	11,6	67	9,8
37	17,8	48	13,7	58	11,4	68	9,7
38	17,3	49	13,5	59	11,2	69	9,5
39	16,9	50	13,2	60	11,0	70	9,4
40	16,5						

Arrow Repair Splicer

Volkmar Hübschmann

Who has not experienced it: The arrow has missed its target and is stuck in the ground near the target. One lifts it up and finds out that the tip is missing. The arrow has most probably hit a stone or some other hard object. The shaft has broken just behind the point.

If one sawed it off and put on a new arrowhead, it would in most cases be too short. With the following simple technique it is possible to repair the arrow without losing any of its length.

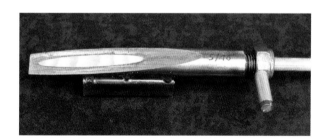

The arrow is fastened in a so-called splicing tube, whereby one must make sure that the annual rings in the wood are exactly horizontal or vertical.

By turning the chuck at the end of the splicing tube, the shaft is clamped fast and is thus fixed immovably for planing.

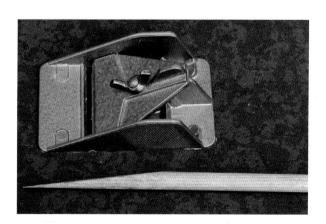

With a suitable plane (small metal block plane or balsa-wood plane) one now planes the splicing surface of the damaged arrow.

The planed surface must be absolutely flat and clean.

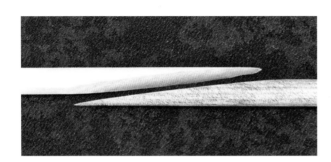

From a piece of an irreparable arrow or a piece of a new arrow shaft, an angled splicing surface is also planed. The procedure here is exactly as described.
The annual rings of this piece must be positioned exactly as those of the arrow to be repaired, so that a harmonious joint results.

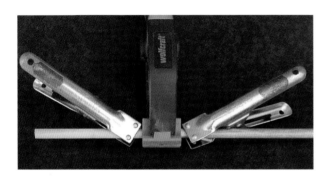

The two identical splicing surfaces are thinly coated with adhesive (watertight wood glue or two-component epoxy resin) and pressed together precisely with clamps.
One can also use plastic clothespins, to which at least the wood glue will not stick. Six or eight of them side by side will provide even pressure.

When the glue has hardened, the repaired area is lightly sanded and the arrow trimmed to the exact length.

After the repaired area has received a water-repellent finish and been fitted with a new point, the arrow is ready for use again.

This type of repair splicing works only on parallel shafts. A splicing tube is always made only for a specific shaft diameter, for which it must fit as exactly as possible.

Tapering of Shafts

Volkmar Hübschmann

Parallel

The wooden shafts available in the archery trade are cylindrical (parallel) and come in diameters of 5/16" (7.9 mm), 11/32" (8.7 mm) and 23/64" (9.1 mm). The diameters of these parallel shafts are the same through their complete length. The shafts are available in various spine values. The spine-value indicates the bending stiffness of the shaft.

The weight of the individual shaft is exactly as influential as the spine value. The shafts within a set of arrows should not show a weight difference of more than one or two grams.

Tapered shafts have a conical shape, meaning that the diameter decreases in certain areas of the shaft.

Single Taper

Various forms of tapered shafts are differentiated:
Single Taper: The shaft tapers in the rear third to the notch end.

Barrel Taper

Barrel Taper: The shaft is divided into three equally long sections (measured from the edge of the arrowhead to the bottom of the notch). The front and rear thirds taper to the point and the notch, the middle third remains parallel. If one leaves the middle third of the shaft unworked, the spine-value changes practically not at all.

Breasted Taper

If one moves the unchanged middle third of the barrel taper backward a little, one calls it a "breasted taper".

Bobtail Taper

Bobtail Taper: The shaft remains parallel for the first 10-12 centimeters (depending on the arrow's length) from the point and then tapers continually to the notch end. This taper makes the shaft some 5# softer compared to a cylindrical, parallel shaft (this value is only a coarse reference point).

The advantages of tapered shafts are:
• The tapering reduces the weight of the shaft in general, and lighter shafts have a flatter trajectory.
• The lesser mass at the end or ends of the shaft makes the swinging movements of the arrow after being shot come to rest sooner; the arrow begins sooner to rotate on its own axis. This makes the arrow fly exactly on its trajectory sooner. In addition, the arrow's speed increases.
• The arrow is more aerodynamic.

Bows that are not cut in the middle and thus have no shooting window, like most wooden bows, are especially good with arrows whose spine-value agrees exactly (paradoxon of archery). Here the tapered shaft can utilize its advantages especially well.

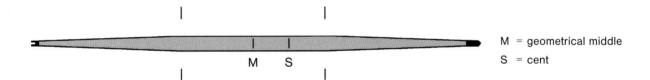

M = geometrical middle
S = cent

The length of the tapered parts of the shaft depends on the arrow's length. The arrow's length in turn depends on the archer's drawing distance; thus the tapering of shafts is a highly individual matter.
Naturally, one can experiment with the lengths of the tapered sections and thus alter the spine-value, the center of gravity (* FOC) and the total weight of the arrow.

Whoever would like o go more deeply into the subject of arrow flight or tuning the arrows/equipment is recommended to consult the book *"Traditionell Tunen"* (see the bibliography in the Appendix).

For one's first individual tests with tapered arrows, I recommend the use of parallel shafts, such as can be bought, and with whose flying behavior one is satisfied.

* The FOC (Forward of Center) term describes the location of the center of gravity before the geometrical center of the arrow.

Tapering in Practice

Whoever does not have a special setup (adjustable planing box, taper-tool) can still make exactly tapered shafts with simple tools.

One needs and angling block (about 5 x 5 cm), on the top of which a V-shaped groove is cut. The length of the block should be such that one can still easily grip the shaft to be worked, so as to be able to turn it while working it.

It is important that the angling block have an attachment for the shaft at one end.

The attachment should be high enough so that a tapered shaft ends even with the attachment. Thus when planing, the bottom of the plane is still guided at the end of the shaft, to prevent making the shaft end into a point.

When the length of the tapered area has been determined, that length is divided into three, and the angling block is marked with tape at the divisions. The shaft is then marked with pencil rings at these tape markings.

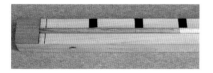

With very thinned spirit stain (applied with a sponge), the shaft is now colored precisely to the first pencil mark. The spirit stain has the advantage of drying in the shortest time. By coloring the shaft, one has a clear view of at which place wood was already taken off, and thus is capable of planing down the entire shaft evenly.

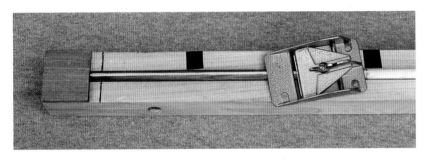

The colored area of the shaft is now planed down evenly all around.
A *Bowyer's-Edge* (see sources) is recommended as a tool. The instructions given here are based on that tool.
Whoever does not have a *Bowyer's-Edge* can work with a balsa plane.

This plane uses a razor blade as a planing iron.
It is important hat the *Bowyer's-Edge* or balsa plane is set so that it takes off only very thin slices of wood.
If 11/32" shafts are being planed down to 5/16", it is normally sufficient to work the shaft in three steps (processes). For thicker shafts, such as 23/64", or when the shaft is to be tapered to less than 5/16", the number of planing processes must be increased. The planing settings used on the plane and the type of the intended taper are decisive.

When the shaft is planed down all around, it is stained again, but this time only the first two thirds.

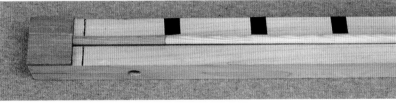

Now this area is again planed down all around, and this work process is also applied to the last third.

After the tapered area has been planed down in three steps, this area of the shaft is smoothed with fine sandpaper or steel wool.
If all the steps have been carried out carefully, the result is an exactly tapered shaft.

Whoever starts to taper shafts does best to make several tests with the individual tapering length and the tool to be used. If one's own way of working leads to satisfactory results, then it is possible to taper a whole set of arrows equally without problems.

Making Arrow Shafts

Volkmar Hübschmann

Making square rough shafts

Many archers spare neither cost nor care to make their bow, but they regard their arrows, in comparison with their bows, as something like stepchildren.
The bow is seen as something permanent, prestigious; the arrows, which get lost or worn, are often seen as second-class.

But it is the arrow that suits the bow and the archer that, depending on the skill of the archer, hits the target, while the bad arrow misses the target or hits it only by chance.
The typical way to obtain arrows is to buy them from a dealer or by mail-order. In a direct purchase, one at least has the chance of looking at the shafts, but if they come by mail, one may be more or less surprised at what one finds as to spine-values, shaft weights, straightness and general quality.

But there are other ways to get shafts. One of them takes you to the nearest wood dealer or lumber-yard. This laborious method, the goal of which is high-value handmade shafts, is what I would like to describe here.
Numerous native woods are suitable for making shafts. I chose birch.

In principle, the same criteria used in selecting wood to make a bow apply here. Sraight growth and grain, as few branches and weaknesses as possible. The wood must also be dry, at least air-dry, meaning that its degree of dampness is that of the air outside.

After I have obtained a birch board four meters long and 5 cm thick from the lumber-yard, I cut it into pieces about 85 cm long with a chain saw.
To make sure that the wood no longer warped from dampness during sawing, the wood dampness was checked.

If the measuring device shows a maximum dampness of 12-15%, then plain right-angled boards are cut and planed (cabinetmaking!)

One end of the boards is always marked with two di-agonal lines. The boards are then cut into small pieces 5 mm square with a circular saw.

If individual pieces are twisted during sawing because the wood was under tension, they are sorted out.
If other faults in the wood appear, they should also be sorted out, or the wood should only be partially worked.

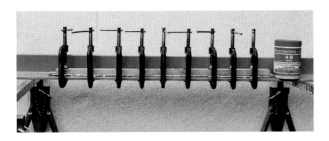

In the next work process, the pieces are turned against each other (those with diagonal annual rings will have a fish-scale pattern on the ends), and glued in the same order in which they were cut from the board.

By gluing the pieces, the different qualities of the wood is largely evened out, the wood becomes more homo-geneous and stable. This has a positive effect on the evenness of spine-values, reflexes and weight.

The small boards are now cut into square (10 x 10 mm) staffs with a band-saw.

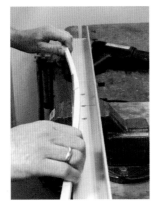

If the square staffs are not completely straight, they should be heated in an angled aluminum profiling rod with a hot-air gun and straightened on a steel bar.

The first goal is reached: straight square raw shafts.

Making a Combined Planing-Barrel Box

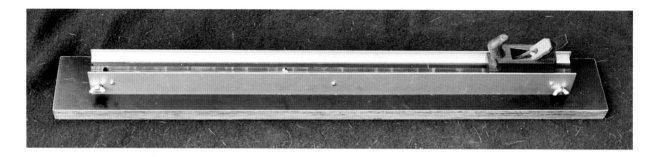

For further working of the raw shafts, either a planing box or a shaft-milling apparatus is recommended.

Planing and barrel boxes are available not only in the USA, but also recently in Germany.

I must say that none of these devices corresponded with my conceptions, so the only alternative was to build my own combined planing/barrel box. The materials for building the box are easy to get, and the choice of an aluminum profiling bar depend on the plane that one intends to use.

My setup in planned not only for small Chinese double planes made by the *Dick* firm, but also for a homemade block plane made according to the functioning principle of the *"Bowyer's-Edge"*.

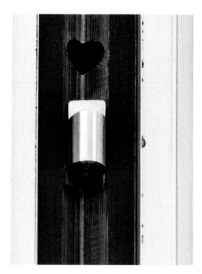

In my setup, the raw shaft rests on a 90-degree V-groove, the middle part of which is cut out of Pertinax. In the groove there are two holes for the adjustable contact pin.

The middle part's height is adjustable at both ends and is fixed at each end in a long hole with a wing bolt and nut.

For exact height adjustment of the middle section from the running rail of the plane, there is an adjustment screw at each end of the box. For planing cylindrical shafts, the middle part is set parallel to the plane rail.

In barrel tapering one can set not only the desired diameter at the ends of the shaft, but also the length of the taper. (In the barrel-taper, only the middle third of the shaft determines the spine-value.) Besides that, there is the possibility of tapering the shaft over almost all of its total length, a so-called bobtail taper, which Howard Hill preferred. Many variations can be made.

The Plane Box in Use

 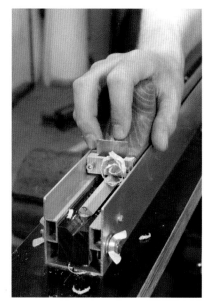

To plane a square shaft into a cylindrical shaft, the box is set for the desired shaft diameter (for example, 9 mm), the contact pin is set in the forward hole, then the angles are planed off evenly and delicately.

Square > octagon > sixteen sides > round.

If the angles are broken roughly or otherwise formed, when the shaft gradually begins to get round, switch to the *"B.-E. Block Plane"*.

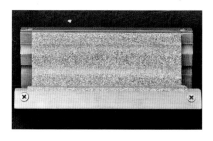 

With a homemade smoothing box (which has two smoothing channels with different diameters) and sandpaper of varying grades, the shaft is smoothed.

The sandpaper is clamped in contact boxes under the angled brass rails by means of metric screws.

Making Arrow Shafts

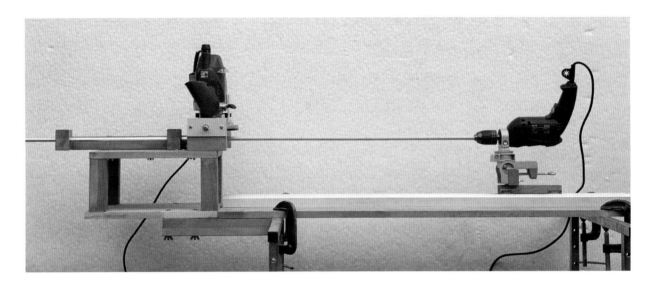

After I had planed some shafts for myself in this manner, I still longed for a quicker and more precise method. I had to have a shaft-milling apparatus.

The principle is similar to that of the planing box. Instead of the plane blade, a fast-turning milling head, driven buy an overhead machine, is used. The square raw shaft is no longer turned by hand, but rather by an electric drill, which moves it past the milling head while turning fast.

If the head is adjusted exactly and the absolutely square raw shaft and the rounded shaft are put in at full length, one gets absolutely round shafts or those with a smooth surface.

When one has already gone to so much trouble with the glued shaft, then in my opinion, a four-way-spliced foreshaft and a reinforced notch must naturally be had along with the barrel-tapered shaft. That's the full program!

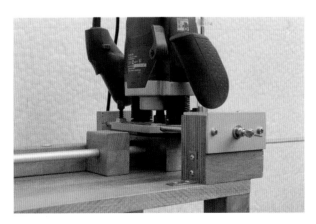

 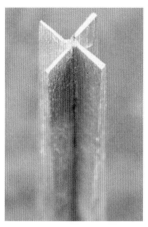

The device shown here was created by Eberhard Kaljumae.

To make multiple splices, I know of two methods:

Method A

Four 90-degree V-shaped grooves are milled into the shaft, 90 degrees apart, angled 2 degrees to the back, and about 12 cm long.

To be able to mill the shaft exactly, one needs a device into which the shaft can be held at the right angle. After each of the four milling procedures, the shaft must be turned exactly 90 degrees.

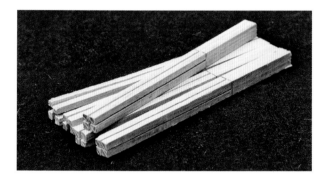

The square foreshaft is sawed in cross-shape to the splicing length.

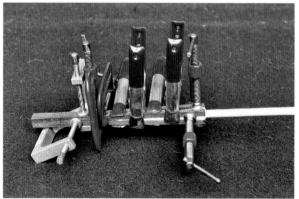

By means of small screw clamps, it is prevented from splitting; the saw cuts are widened with small wedges, and the milled shaft, to which glue is applied, is pushed into the foreshaft.

The splice is kept in clamps until the glue has hardened.

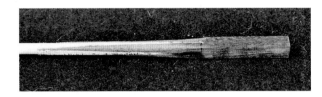

Making a fourfold splice is relatively uncomplicated, but fitting the square foreshaft exactly onto the round shaft is somewhat more difficult.

A simple wood block with a V-shaped groove and an attachment as well as a Japanese fine saw and Japanese radius plane give good service here. For the last steps of the work, the shaft is put into the planing box again, and is then rotated in the smoothing box by the electric drill.

Method B

One also needs an (aluminum) block that holds the shaft, but the shaft is held at a different angle. With a 45-degree miller, identical splicing joints are milled into the shaft and the foreshaft.

After the spliced areas have been treated with glue and stuck together, they are wrapped with a strong rubber band until the glue is dry.

Pressing the splice together with a rubber band also works very well in Method A.

Note:
Method B is somewhat more demanding in milling, but is clearly faster. The splicing length, based on a shaft diameter of 9 mm, measures 11 cm in my shafts made with Method A, 7.5 cm with Method B. Method A produces more decorative foreshafts. Thus both methods have their minor pluses and minuses.

If one uses hard and stable wood such as locust or rosewood for the foreshafts, this considerably increases the life span of an arrow. The arrows are much stronger right behind the points, thus at the place where they like to break off.

After the foreshaft is spliced on, the shaft is shortened to the desired length.

At a right angle to the notch or parallel to the glued seam in a glued shaft, the shaft is sawed 2 cm long; the resulting saw-cut should be about 3 mm wide.
A strip of hardwood (or horn, bone, etc.) is glued into this cut.

I use thick oak veneer, which I have soaked for a time in black wood stain. The inlay should project some-what over the wood, to be cut down smooth after the lime dries.

Now the time has come to be concerned about the shaft's spine-value. The shaft is laid on the spine-tester with the glued joint vertical and measured.

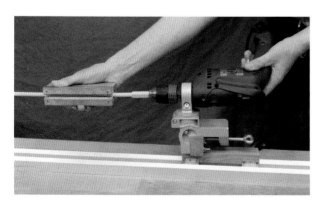

An overly stiff shaft is decreased in diameter evenly until the desired spine-value is attained.

To do that, the shaft is held in the drilling machine and smoothed with the grinding block. If the difference is too great, it can also be worked with the *"B. E. Block Plane"* in the planing box.

Making Arrow Shafts

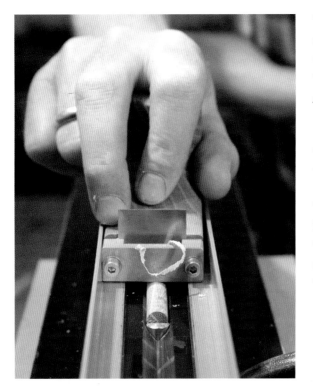

The planing box is set to the desired diameter at the shaft ends and the length of the taper, the attachment pin is paced in the hole intended for tapering, and the shaft is planed and turned until the *"B. E. Block plane"* takes off no more wood.

Finally, cut out the notch again and smooth everything again with fine sandpaper or steel wool—and the shaft is ready!

The following work processes on the way to finishing the arrow, such as painting, sealing the surface, feathering, wrapping and attaching the point, are now merely minor matters compared to the work that one has already done.

You can be just as proud of these arrows as you can of a good self-made bow!

I must admit, though, that at the beginning it made me feel uneasy to shoot these arrows, for one might, of course, lose or damage one . . .

Arrow Straightener

Volkmar Hübschmann

Wooden arrows have the unpleasant ability to warp. Even if the arrow was straight to begin with, from shooting itself, from variations in the wood moisture of the shaft, or because the arrow somehow had a hard landing from a shot—there are many reasons why a wooden arrow bends.

Such bent arrows, though, can be straightened again by means of meat and pressure. The arrow is warmed at the bent place (for example, with a hot-air gun), and then straightened. With an arrow straightener, pressure can be applied to the bent spot.

My arrow straightener is made out of an old bicycle saddle support and a small brass roller. The brass roller has a groove in the middle; its radius is roughly equal to the diameter of a shaft. The saddle support is cut off at its lower end and has a hole bored through it. In this hole there is a bolt that serves as an axle for the roller.

The heated shaft is laid on a flat surface (such as a tabletop), and the arrow straightener is run strongly over the bent spot.
If the shaft is strongly warped, it is bent in the opposite direction of the bend to and beyond the point where it is straight. A side effect of this is that the whole shaft is nicely polished in this way.

A simple but effective tool that can be made without much trouble.

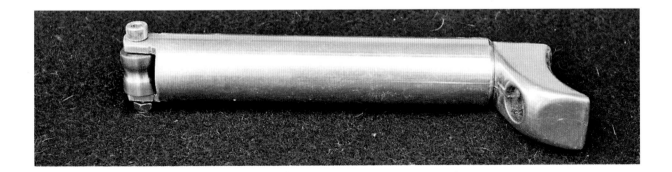

Shaft Working

Herbert Müller

I buy only spun and weighed shafts, which must be exactly straight because of my *Crestings* work.

After I have gathered a group of shafts with spine-values and weights as equal as possible (if possible, to within half a gram), I saw the individual shafts to the right dimensions for me.

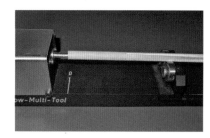

For this I use the *"Arrow-Multi-Tool"*, for in this device, practically all the functions that I need during arrow-making are united.
First I set up the desired length in inches, using the measuring slider.

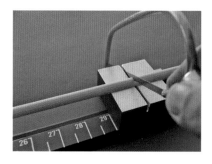

Then I place the shaft on the left block and saw it with an ordinary store-bought little bow saw that can be used easily in the sawing slit of the measuring slider. Thus it is assured that all the shafts come out the same length and no shaft is sawed at an angle.

To prepare for staining and treating with the wax glaze, the shafts are dampened with water (small sponges), so that the fibers stand up. After drying, the shafts are smoothed with fine (600 grain) sandpaper.

I remove the sanding dust with a soft, dry cloth.

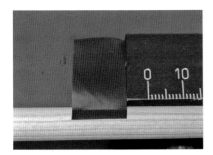

Now I measure about nine inches (23 cm) on the Arrow-Tool, set the hand layout accordingly, and stick a small piece of masking tape to the shaft. The front part is treated with a teak-colored wax glaze that gives the shaft a bright and warm brown tone. The back part is stained in color.

To have a good, even dividing line between the brown and colored parts, I tape off the shafts.

Before the painting of the shafts begins, I make the cone for the notch at the end of the shaft.

The shaft is pointed by putting it in the right sharpening tool by hand and turning it, as when sharpening a pencil. When the blade takes off no more wood, the right cone has been made.

If the arrow is to be fitted with a glued-on point, I must now make the cone for the point as well.

The well-shaken wax glaze for the forward part of the arrow is now applied with a brush.

If need be, this can also be thinned with water, which makes it easier to apply and does not immediately penetrate so deeply into the wood.

Thinned stains can be spread well with paper towels. If the shaft is brushed, I press the paper towel onto the shaft so firmly that it does not tear but the shaft can still slide through the paper. Masking tape prevents the rear part of the shaft from becoming dirtied with wax glaze.

If a very dark brown tone should be desired, the brushing and wiping can be repeated as often as one wants. One should just let the glaze have a little time to soak into the wood before applying the next coat.

Now the masking tape is removed and the shaft is stained.

I have had very good experience with the Clou firm's stains, both the water-soluble and alcohol-soluble types. When painting, one must just be sure to make the first coat with a paint that contains a solvent, except the white universal wood stain, since the stain will otherwise smear or dissolve into the paint pigment.

When I make arrows with two-colored ends (the rear end is always white), I first apply a coat of very flexible boat lacquer over the stain, let it dry at least 24 hours, sand it down briefly and then finish the cresting.

Then come two coats of acrylic paint over the shaft, so that everything is well protected. Since I use paintbrushes made by the Edding company, I cannot use any paint that contains solvents, for this would dissolve and ruin the paint.

When the stains and glaze are thoroughly dry, the notch is glued on ("Fletch-Tite" or all-purpose glue). Unlike the cut notches, plastic notches have the advantage of being easy to replace if they are damaged or hit.

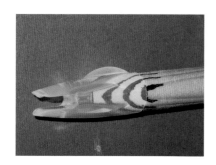

Depending on the style of the arrow—for example, plastic notches would not do on a historical or medieval arrow—all the plastic notches on the market can be fitted.

They exist in full color or semitransparent, marbleized, with and without side flags, which is intended for use without sight control.

When a plastic notch is fitted, one must be sure to get the right position of the notch in respect to the grain of the wood, just as when sawing a notch. The notch must be glued on so that the slit is at a right angle to the grain (the annual rings).

I have colored the annual rings for the photos, so as to show their course better.

On the notch cone (the pointed rear end of the shaft), a little glue is applied. Then the notch is carefully pushed onto the cone and turned back and forth a couple times, to spread the glue around evenly.

The small flag on the side is placed parallel to the annual rings. A marking on the shaft helps to find the right position. The notch must stay in this position until the glue has hardened.

Finally the notch is pushed moderately firmly onto the shaft in the direction of the point. Any glue that oozes out can be carefully removed with a finger. This has the effect of more or less "sealing" the joint between the notch and the wood.

After fiting a few notches, one knows the right amount of glue to use, and so it will happen more and more rarely that glue is squeezed out from under the notch. The perfect amount is enough so that when the notch is pushed forward, the glue comes exactly to the rim of the notch.

Then I screw the point onto the shaft.

Sometimes it happens that the shaft is raised up somewhat by the glaze and thus the point canot be set on.
In this case I use an old jelly glass to roll and compress the shaft in the area where the point fits on.

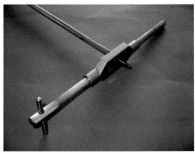

For screwing the point on, I use special pliers, with which I can hold the point more firmly, and then turn the shaft until I feel that the wood has come all the way forward in the point.

In the next step I apply the first coat of clear paint. Since in this case I use only white UHB (Universal-Holz-Beize made by Clou), I can work exclusively with acrylic paint. With the brush I apply the well-shaken paint evenly. I let the first coat dry a long time.

Then I draw the shaft through P600 grain sandpaper some four or five times, to make the surface smooth, for the smoother it is, better-looking and more even the cresting rings will be.

Painting Arrows With Legos

Georg Kloss

Traditional archery is more fun with self-painted wooden arrows. Without technical aids, though, one must have a very steady hand to get good results.

With Legos it is easy, precise and economical. I have found the parts in the long-since abandoned Lego kits of my children.
If the appropriate Lego material is not at hand, one can also build his arrow-painting device out of other materials. On www.1000steine.de one can find all Lego parts with catalog numbers and dimensions.

• The left hand rolls the arrow, which lays between the axles, away from the body (to the front).
• The right hand guides the paintbrush with the paint on it slowly onto the arrow from above. The brush is moved smoothly between the angled roof stones.
• Left-handed people simply do it the opposite way.

Wooden and Rubber Parts
• A wooden plate 8 x 32 cm, 12 mm thick
• 82 cm long wooden board, 5 x 24 mm, rounded on one side, cut right-angled (not beveled),
  attached to the wooden plate with brass nails and wood glue, corners rounded with sandpaper.
• a rubber plate some 25 x 25 mm, glued under the wooden plate to prevent skidding.

Lego Parts
• Two ground plates 8 x 16 cm, 9.6 cm thick, gray,
• A linking plate with 4 x 8 knobs, 3.2 mm thick, blue,
• Four building stones with 4 knobs, 3.2 mm thick, red, under all four axles,
• Two building stones with 4 knobs, 3.2 mm thick, red, under the small axles,
• Two big auto axles, 4.8 cm long, on the white building stones with 4 knobs, wheel diameter 25 mm (other Lego axles can also be used. They must not move when turned.)
• Two small auto axles, 3.5 cm long, on the white and red building stones with 4 knobs, wheel diameter 20 mm.
• Four building stones with 8 knobs, 9.6 mm thick, red, for the brush rack,
• Two diagonal roof stones, with 4 knobs below and 2 above, red, to guide the brush smoothly.

All parts are secured with *"Arrow-Mate Cement"*.

Paints and Brushes
I use *"Acryl Hobby Line"* matte paint and *"Hobby Line"* brushes from a paint shop.

A clear primer improves the results.
Well-hardening wax or colorless paint will protect the beautiful painting.

Cresting

Herbert Müller

"Wow! Are they beautiful! But they are much too good for shooting!"
I often get to hear such expressions.
Cresting is one of many possible ways to create individualized arrows.

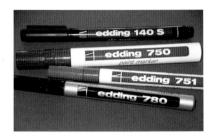

For the colored rings around the shaft, I find the Edding markers of series 140, 750, 751 and 780 ideal.

From the 140 series I use an S-width marker for the black dividing lines; the others have varying widths and thus work for me for all widths that I use for cresting. They also have the advantage that there is always enough fluid on the tip and an even application is thus guaranteed.

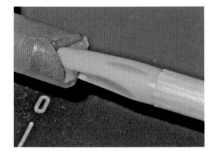

After the first painting and smoothing of the surface (see the Shaft Working chapter), I now use my cresting machine.

For this, the notch-holder is screwed onto the axle of the motor. This bracket is so conceived that the notch stays firmly attached and, at the same time, is turned while centered on the axle.

The arrow is stuck onto the notch-holder and laid on the holder with the two rollers.

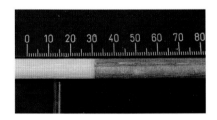

I set up the hand-bracket with the millimeter scale after the beginning of the cresting.

I always begin at the transition from the stained part to the brown fore-shaft. I "hide" this transition under a ring 10 mm wide in all.

To the left of it, at a distance of 20 mm at most, I make another such ring, and these two form the connection of the rear part of the arrow to the front part.

The cresting machine, of course, has a transformer for regulation, but I only use the slowest step. On this stage the arrow always turns quickly enough.

An advantage, as I see it, is the possibility of making the arrow rotate either toward me or away from me. I prefer, depending on how I hold the marker, to have it turn away from me. The shaft turns in the applicating direction of the marker tip.

In the first step, I paint the black dividing lines with the watertight marker with "S" point (very fine) of the Edding 140 Series markers. Since the arrow is turning very evenly, I need only put the marker on it and hold it until the ring is closed. Of course no deviations to the right or left should occur, or there will be a snaky line.

My first rings were not as they are today, for it is true here as elsewhere that one is not born a master; practice makes perfect. With every set of arrows, the lines become finer.

By using the millimeter scale, it is not difficult to measure equal distances.

The number and arrangement of the rings depend absolutely on personal taste, so that there is no point to citing certain measurements here. There are no limits to one's individual creativity. An arrow should not be overloaded with cresting, not overly colorful. Besides, traces of use will make themselves known in time, and then a beautiful cresting will suffer.

In the colored rings I always try to establish a relationship to the shaft colors or at least the feather colors. This results in a harmonious total color scheme. I like o make the two outer decorative rings silver, gold or bronze-colored. This depends on what colors the shaft and the feathers have. Silver always goes well and looks neutral. Gold and bronze do not go as well with certain color tones as silver does. But in the end, it is the archer's decision.

For the rings on the shaft, I often write down the scale values for the beginning and end of the dividing rings, so hat these are the same on every arrow.

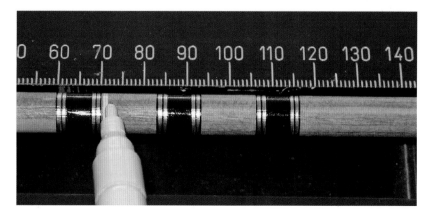

For the wide inner rings, I usually choose black, because for one thing, it goes well with silver, and for another, it makes a good contract with the brown of the foreshaft.

The procedure is the same as with the dividing rings, only that the Edding 7XX Series markers need to be shaken well before they are used.

Then I do not press the marker right on the dividing line, but slightly to the side. When this turning is finished, I approach the edge by moving the marker until the color ends neatly at the dividing line. After that I move the marker farther in the direction of the opposite dividing line, and when there is no more wood visible between the color and the dividing line, I carefully lift the marker off.

At first it often happened that I then made a move to the outside and painted through the dividing line. So it is best to move the marker away from the dividing line.

When the forward area has had cresting applied, I put a feather in the bracket, stick the arrow into the feathering apparatus, and put the adhesive on the arrow dry.

Now I mark, with a soft pencil, the places where the splices feather will go, at which the shaft will be given colored stripes.

Since I do not give the feathers a wrapping, I mark the beginning and end of the feathering on the shaft with narrow rings, showing the optical beginning and end of the feathering.

Then the shaft is painted with the desired cresting. Additional colored bands that are to run around the shaft are painted with the chosen colors.

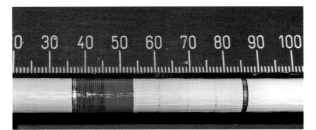

For such colored bands, like those of a rainbow arrow, I use a pencil to mark the width of a stripe, for here a black dividing line would be only a disturbance.

When all the creating bands are applied, the shaft is given its second coat, and after that dries, its third coat.

Now the shaft can be feathered. Before gluing the feathers on, I arrange these in the adhesive according to the cresting stripes, so that the stripes in the feather exactly match the stripes on the shaft.

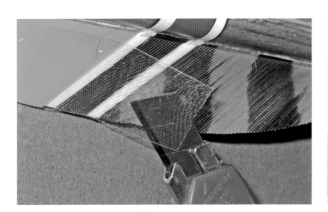

After the adhesive dries—I leave every arrow for an hour with the adhesive on the shaft—the band of Tesa adhesive that has held the individual parts of the feather splice is carefully lifted and removed with the blade of a modeling knife.

For the last step, I add a drop of glue at the beginning of every feather quill, so that if an arrow hits the ground, the quill will not loosen from the shaft or be torn off.

After this drop has dried, the arrow goes into the quiver and will hopefully always hit its target.

Wrapping Arrows

Volker Alles

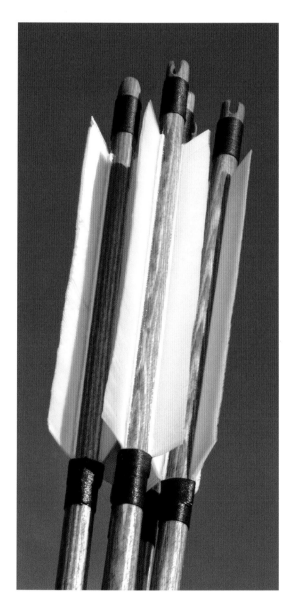

Almost every archer has already experienced one of these two situations, or at least seen it happen to someone else:

a) One misses a target, the arrow slides across the ground, and one feather is completely missing, or grass or the like has been caught under the half-loosened quill.

b) One shoots a primitive bow, using his index finger or the back of his hand as the arrow rest, and after the shot he has a scratch, or worse, there.

What can be done about it?
For the second situation, one simply raises the nocking point a few millimeters or holds the bow correspondingly lower.
For both situations, wrapping is recommended to hold the feather quills securely on the arrow shaft.

For millennia, this has been done all over the world, and it is no only functional, but also looks good. At first one's thick fingers will have some trouble with the thin thread, but with some practice, one can make every wrapping within a minute, I promise!

Lefthanders will naturally have to do everything in mirror-image form.

Wrapping Arrows

The three feathers have, as before, been glued to the shaft, but this time the bristles have been cut off the quill for some five millimeters, or simply pulled off frontward. For an elegant transition, it also helps to cut the quill somewhat flatter, closer to the shaft, at this place. For all cutting work on feathers, a razor-sharp knife is absolutely necessary; otherwise the results will not look good.

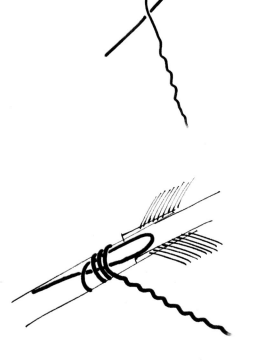

1. One cuts a piece of thread about 80 to 100 cm long from a spool; this varies according to the length of the wrapping and the thickness of the thread; one takes the thread in one's left hand so that the rest of it hangs out, and holds the arrow under one's left shoulder not far from the point, so that the feathered end is in front of one's face.

Now one makes a loop about 3 cm long around the shaft, so that half of the loop is between two feather quills.

2. With the left thumb, press the loop onto the shaft at the crossing point, and with the left hand, wrap the thread four times clockwise (as viewed from the notch) fairly tightly over the loop and shaft.

3. As shown in the picture, pull sideways on the loop, so that the thread at the beginning of the loop runs from the beginning of the loop to the first wrapping. As long as the long piece of thread is held tightly, these first wrappings will fix the loop, and in addition, the wrapping will not loosen again from the front when one continues to wrap from the back.

Does all this sound complicated? It is only as long as one has no practice, but one has already done the hardest part of it.

4. With the fingers of the right hand, one holds the thread tightly and turns the arrow with the left hand.

In this way, the thread runs through the right hand and wraps itself evenly around the shaft, one turn after another, always covering more of the shaft, and finally wraps automatically around the feather quill.

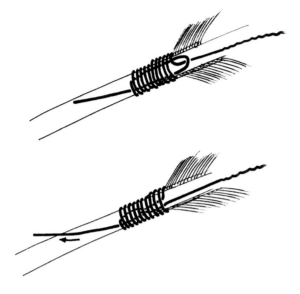

5. When the wrapping has thus reached the bristles of the feather, one feeds the end of the thread through the remainder of the loop, which still looks out from under the wrapping.

6. And now comes the catch to it: Hold the end of the wrapping with the left hand, and pull firmly with the right hand on the beginning of the wrapping, which runs under the wrapping.

Thus the loop becomes smaller, until it slides under the wrapping. Thus it takes the upper end of the thread with it under the wrapping, where this has also become a loop.

The two ends of the thread are thus hooked together under the wrapping but can no longer get loose from each other, because the wrapping is on top of them. If one has wrapped too loosely and the thread is stable, one can still pull on the two projecting ends of the thread and tighten the ends. Finished!

If one has wrapped tightly enough, the entire wrapping holds itself right, and a following application of glue or paint will just make it all the more secure and help keep dirt off it.

By the same method, one absolutely must bind the self-cut notches on one's shafts below the notch slit, to prevent splitting.
It is really surprising how much force such a wrapping can take.

Whoever fears that the hooked-together thread ends will come loose under the wrapping can wrap his shafts according to the principle described in wrapping the middle of the bowstring. There the ends of the thread are held under the first and last circuits of the wrapping and thus covered somewhat better, but not held quite so securely.

Leather Broadhead

Juergen Knoll

Ready-made blunt arrowheads made of metal or rubber can be bought, but one can also make them oneself by simple means.

In combination with strongly braking Flu-Flus, one can shoot with these blunt arrows at, for example, helium-filled balloons without always breaking them. When shooting in a sport hall, leather broadheads leave no ugly scratches on the floor, as a rubber broadhead will do.

Cartridge shells of various calibers.

Needed Materials
• One .38 caliber special or 357 Magnum shotgun cartridge case (for 11/32" shaft diameters).
• One 32 caliber cartridge case (for 5/16" shaft diameters). Simply ask at the nearest gun club if
  someone has such empty cases; that usually works.
• One piece of leather 50 x 50 mm, 3 to 5 mm thick.
• Linen cord or art twine.

Needed Tools
• A sharp knife, such as a scalpel.
• A cutting board.
• A punch or punch pliers.

Left: store-bought rubber and steel broadheads.

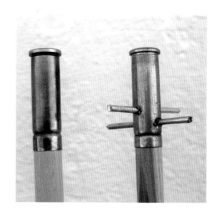

Right: Homemade cartridge-case broadheads, with crossed nails at the far right to prevent the arrow from sliding under a cut in the grass. (Photos: Bernd Neuffler)

1. Cut the leather.

2. Angle the lashings so that they will not turn out to be too thick.

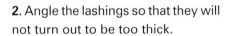

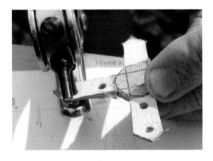

3. Make two holes in each lashing.

4. Moisten the leather briefly under the water faucet.

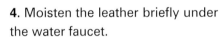

5. Feed the thread through the holes.

6. Stick the shaft into the cartridge case and place it on the center of the leather.

If you want to fasten the broadhead directly to the arrow, you can also glue the case on, with hot glue or another glue of your choice.

7. Pull the lashings together with the cord and even them up.

8. Begin wrapping at the thick part of the broadhead and wrap until just before the end of the cartridge case.

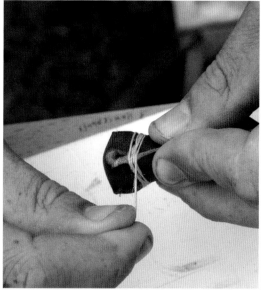

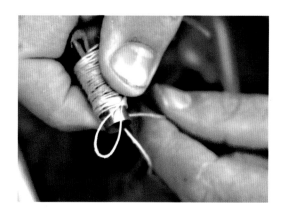

9. If you would like to make a supply of leather broadheads, tie the wrapping and leave about one meter of cord there.

10. You can trim off the protruding ends of the broadhead.

11. Now you can take this broadhead off the shaft and store it.

12. When you want to attach this broadhead to a shaft, glue the cartridge case onto the shaft, simply wrap 1 to 2 cm of the cord around the shaft, and then pull the threads under the wrapping. Finally, one can brush a little *UHU Resin* onto the wrapping and the broadhead is ready.

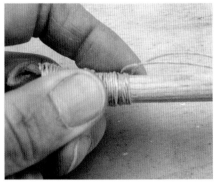

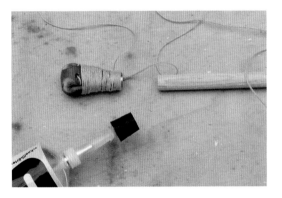

Even though the arrow looks quite harmless with a broadhead, one should never forget that blunt arrows are also dangerous.
They always used to be used for hunting small game, and can result in injuries. So always be careful, as you would with a "real" arrowhead.

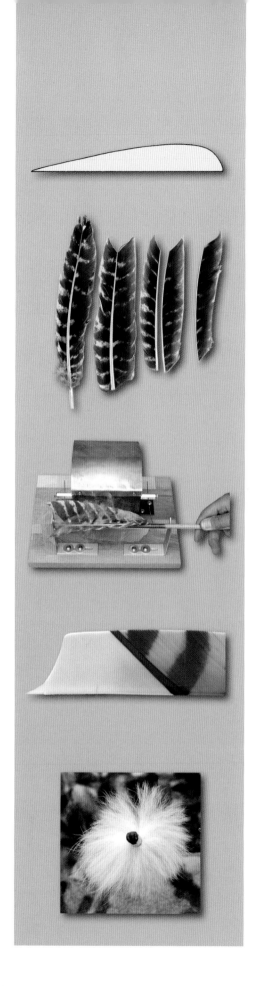

Feathering Arrows

Basics of Feathering Arrows

Materials and Tools for Feathering

Building Your Own Feathering Device

Cutting Feathers

Feather Burners

De Luxe Feathering

Flu-Flu Arrows

Tracers

Basics of Feathering Arrows

Volkmar Hübschmann

Upper part of the feather

Bristles

Quill

Lower part of the feather

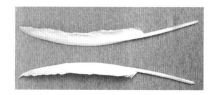

In principle, all feathers are suitable for feathering arrows, as long as they are big enough.

The feathers sold in archery shops are almost exclusively turkey feathers, but goose feathers and, for example, swan feathers, are also well suited for feathering.

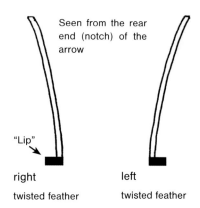

Seen from the rear end (notch) of the arrow

"Lip"

right
twisted feather

left
twisted feather

The feathers from the right and left wings of a bird are not the same; they differ in that feathers from the left side are twisted to the left, and those from the right side are twisted to the right.

This is true only of the upper part of the feather. The lower part of the feather (which it is sometimes possible to use) is always twisted opposite to the upper part.

It does not matter at all whether right- or left-twisting feathers are used for feathering. But one must never use right- and left-twisted feathers together on one arrow.

So it is very important that an arrow may be feathered with only one sort of feathers!

f one is not sure whether it is a right or left feather, one observes the feather from behind, as if it were attached to an arrow, from the notch end.

The bristles of a feather meet the quill evenly on one side; on the opposite side the quill is somewhat over them, making a sort of "lip". If the "lip" is one the left side (seen from the notch end), then it is a right feather, and conversely—"lip" on the right side, left feather.

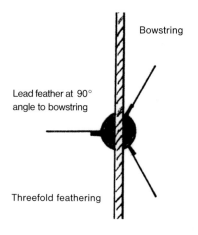

Bowstring

Lead feather at 90° angle to bowstring

Threefold feathering

As a rule, a feather is feathered with three equally long feathers (exceptions" Flu-Flu arrows, and two- or fourfold feathered arrows).

In threefold feathering, one must make sure that the so-called lead feather is at a right angle to the bowstring.

The color of the feathers also plays a role. Light feathers make it easy for the archer to observe the flight of the arrow; the trajectory of the arrow makes a clearer impression (very important when learning to shoot instinctively!); in addition, the landing spot on the target is more recognizable, and lost arrows are easier to find.

But the real task of the feathers is to stabilize the arrow. The feathering increases the air resistance at the rear end of the arrow. Along with the spine-value of the shaft and the location of the center of gravity, the feathering is decisive for an arrow's correct flight.

The length of the feathers or, better stated, the surface area of the feathers, has to suit the arrow, in terms of the arrow's weight and in a certain way also the shooting performance of the bow. A light flight arrow (a special arrow for long shooting) or an arrow for a weak child's bow needs less feathering than, for example, a heavy medieval war arrow, which was shot from a corresponding bow. As a rule of thumb, the heavier the arrow, the larger the feathering must be.

In general, one can say that larger feathers stabilize the arrow more quickly and balance the archer's shooting errors. The disadvantage of larger feathers, of course, is that they use up energy and thus make the arrow fly more slowly.

For our purposes, the "normal" traditional tournament shooting with bows whose pulling weights are roughly between 35 and 60 pounds, and for arrow weights around 30 grams, a feather length of about five inches (12.7 cm) should be fully sufficient.

Most store-bought feathering devices set the limit of feather length at about 6 inches (ca. 16 cm).

One also has the choice of using straight or spiral feathering. In straight feathering, the feather is mounted on the shaft almost straight, displaced only by about the width of the quill. In spiral feathering, the feather is wound around the shaft and thus attached (like the spiral of a drill).

For spiral feathering, one needs special curved clamps for the feathering device. Left-twisted feathers can be attached only with a left spiral, right-twisted feathers—logically—only with a right spiral.

A spiral feathering makes the arrow rotate on its own axis, the arrow stabilizes itself more quickly and generally has a more stable flight. Of course spiral feathering, like a greater feather area, also uses up energy. The energy loss with spiral feathering, though, is not as serious, and as I see it, one can gladly take it in the bargain to gain a more stable flight.

When one considers the factors mentioned here, it is not difficult to find the feathering most suitable for one's own arrows, bow and shooting style, and there is enough space left for the creative formation of the feathers as well.

Materials and Tools for Feathering

Volkmar Hübschmann

There are several ways to obtain feathers. The simplest way is to buy them in an archery shop. Naturally, one can also get feathers from farmers or poultry growers and do all the work oneself.

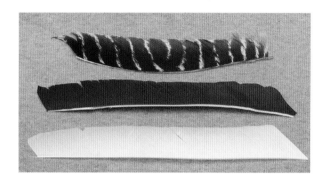

In an archery shop there are feathers for sale that are worked to the point that they need only be glued onto the shaft. One can choose among various shapes, lengths and colors.

If one wants to decide the form of his heathers himself, there are so-called "full-length feathers" available in the trade, meaning feathers with their quills already split and smoothed.

Here are various methods of bringing feathers into shape:

1. One makes patterns in the desired feather shape, for example, out of strong cardboard and cuts the feathers according to these patterns with sharp (!) haircutting scissors. This method is very economical, but it is unfortunately not the most precise.

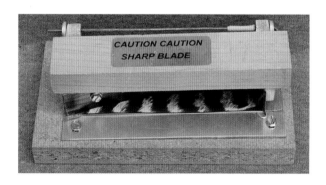

2. One buys a feather stamp, in which the feather is laid and stamped out by striking on the upper part of the stamp (in which the stamping knife is fitted).

The result is an exactly cut feather. The disadvantages are that one is limited to one feather shape, and that feather stamps are not exactly cheap.

3. One burns the feathers into shape with a glowing wire. One would have to build the feather burner himself, for as far as I know, such a device is on the market only in the USA.
The advantage is the complete freedom in forming the feather. One can "burn" all shapes that one can twist wire into out of the burner. The "burned" feathers are all completely the same and exact. One should, though, use the feather burner only outside in the fresh air, for it produces a fairly strong smell.

In my view, such a homemade feather burner is unbeatable in terms of price and performance.

For those who want to shape feathers themselves, I have drawn 1:1 scale feather patterns (shown on the next page).

To glue the feathers on, it is sensible to use a feathering device. Especially capable arrow-makers can do without one, but in the long run the investment thoroughly pays for itself.

These devices are available in the trade in a fairly wide variety.
With most of them, one can feather only a single shaft, but there are multiple feathering devices, with which one can feather several shafts simultaneously (which I think only pays when one must prepare large quantities of arrows quickly, or for groups or clubs).

Before obtaining a feathering device, one must decide on the type of feathering (straight, left or right spiral) that one wants.
You can build a feathering device yourself, though, at least for straight feathering.

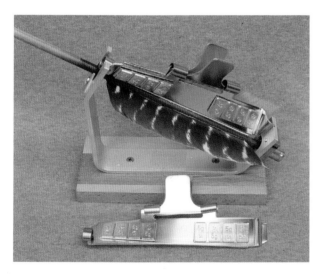

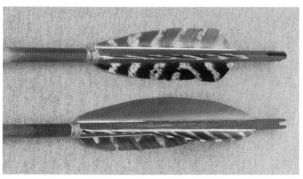

Securing the feathering by wrapping it at the front end avoids injury to the back of one's hand (especially important for archers who shoot directly over the back of the hand) and prevents the feathers from loosening. (See "Wrapping Arrows" chapter)

Materialsl and Tools for Feathering

Feather shapes as models in 1 : 1 scale, 5-inch (12.7 cm) feathers

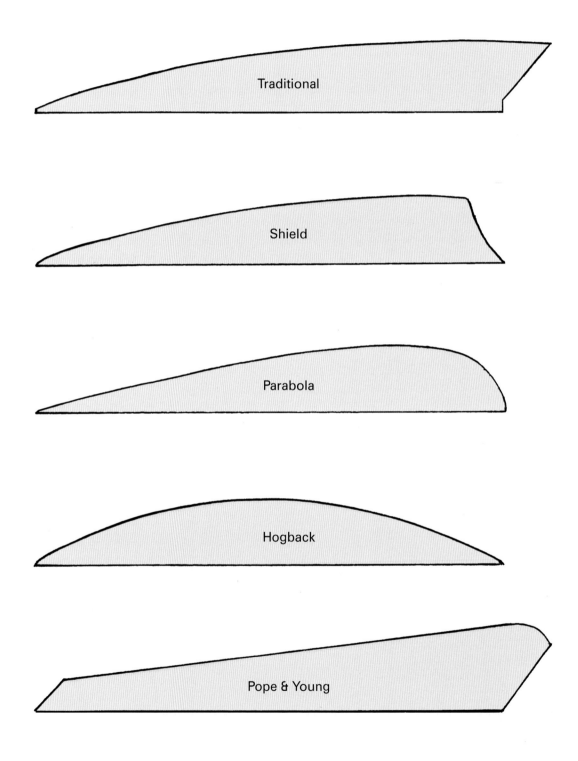

Traditional

Shield

Parabola

Hogback

Pope & Young

Materialsl and Tools for Feathering

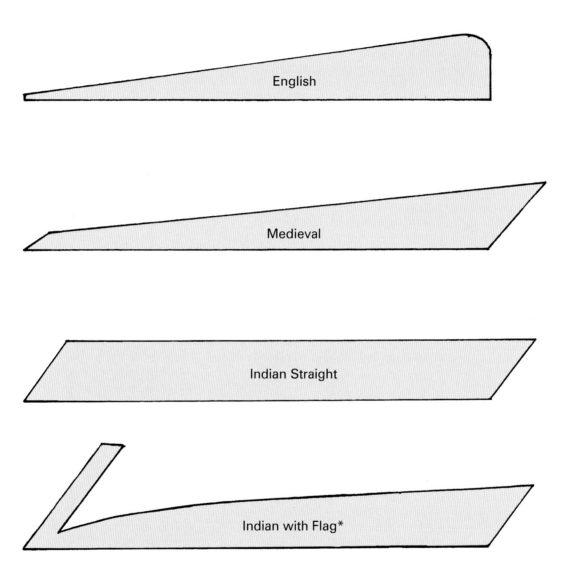

English

Medieval

Indian Straight

Indian with Flag*

(* the first bristles were not cut)

By using these patterns, one can make one's own patterns or bend wires for a feather burner. Naturally, these shapes can be varied according to one's own needs and conceptions.

Building Your Own Feathering Device

Heinrich Prell

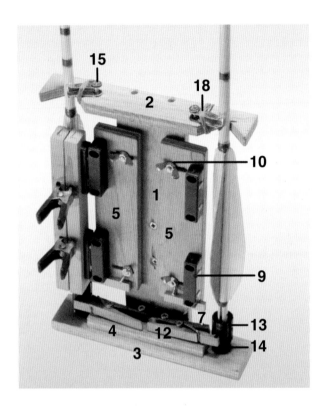

Materials	No.	Dimension in mm
1. Middle part	1	25 x 60 x 10
2. Upper arrow channel	1	180 x 30 x 10
3. Base	1	180 x 40 x 10
4. Base riser	1	110 x 19 x 10
5. Adjusting surfaces	2	160 x 40 x 10
6. Support	1	160 x 40 x 10
7. Feather clamp	2	20 x 10 x 10
8. Feather clamp blocks	4	160 x 19 x 12
9. Magnetic snapper	4	48 x 19 x 13
10. Set-screw	4	M4 x 30
Wing nut	4	M4 x 30
11. Metal clamp	4	52 x 19 x 12
12. Clothespin clamps	2	
13. Notch holder	2	*Pattex* tube caps
14. Mount for #13	2	*UHU* tube caps
15. Arrow-pushing lever	2	
16. Notch pin	1	diameter 3.5 x 19
17. Spax screws	20	diameter 3.5 x 15
18. Rubber rings	2	

Here I show you my feathering device (max. 6") that you can build.
The material needs are fairly meager and easy to obtain. As can be seen at once in the pictures, the device is designed to hold two arrows. The expense is a little greater, but feathering can be done twice as fast.

The device stands slightly tilted to the back (15 degrees). The shafts are stuck into the turnable notch holders at the bottom, and pressed into the prismatic cuts on top by means of a small pushing lever.
Glue is applied to the feathers placed in the feather clamps. Then the whole thing is pressed against the shaft through the use of two magnetic snappers.

Details:

No. 1-7 consist of 10 mm thick plywood. A piece measuring 350 x 25 mm is enough to saw, if necessary, even the feather clamp blocks out of. After that, it is best to begin with the 45-degree cuts on #2.

Then place #2 even with the rear edge on the base #3 and, with a sharp pencil, draw the angles of the cutouts on #3. When you then place a piece of arrow shaft on the marked cutout, draw its circumference and drill a 3-mm hole exactly in the middle, you have the middle of the mount (#14) for the notch holder (#13).

The mount (#14) consists here of a tube cap, such as from *UHU-Resin* or *Alleskleber* glue. From the tube side out, the threading has to be scraped out from inside some 8 mm deep (about the length of the threading) with a small knife.

With a Spax screw, the tube threading is screwed on centrally from below through the 3-mm hole, and fixed in place with epoxy resin glue (such as UHU-plus endfest 300, the cap of which is also suitable, but the other way around with the tube end out).

The notch holder (#13) to hold the shaft consists of a *Pattex* tube cap, which has twelve angles with a high profile and is thus suitable for 2-, 3-, 4- and 6-fold feathering.

One of the edges is chosen as the leading feather point, and at 90 degrees to it, or three edges farther, a 2.5-mm hole is bored 10 mm from the lower edge of the cap.

I have used a piece of a 50 nail here, which I hammered fairly flat and then glued in the hole, turned suitably for my notches. You should test in advance what diameter and what height fit your notches best.

If you use notches with indicator profiles, you must cut a small notch in the notch holder at this point with a small knife or hot wire.

If you should have no empty Pattex or UHU tubes in the house, ask friends or neighbors. I have found that a few dried-out tubes can be found in almost every household, usually far to the back of a drawer.

Building Your Own Feathering Device

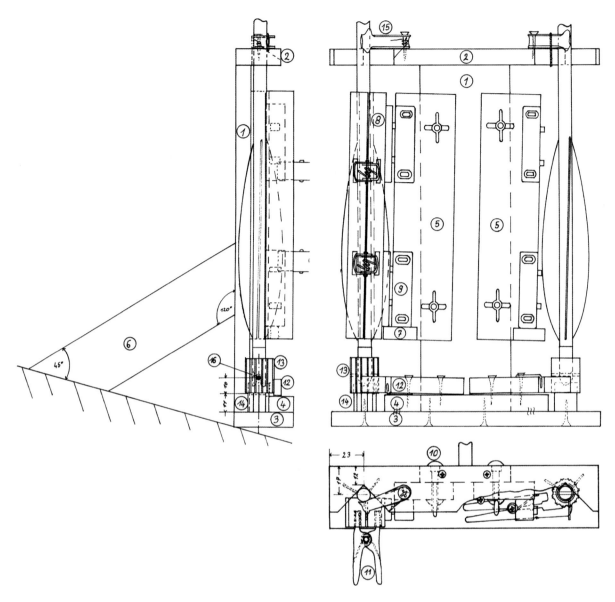

When you have finished the notch holder, screw or glue the base riser (#4) in the middle, and with the front edge even, onto the base (#3). Then shorten two wooden clothespins as shown in the drawing. With a file you can shape the longer points of the pins exactly like the profile of the Pattex cap. The clothespins are screwed to the base riser with a screw through the spiral spring; thus you determine the position of the notch to the leading feather.

The pressure of the clothespins on the notch holder should be as big as possible, and is attached to the rear arm with a second screw with the pin open.

The arrow shaft should be pushed later, lightly and with only a little friction, into the upper channel (#2). Here I have used the sheet-metal arm of a tipping peg, the point of which I curved into a nose with flat pliers. The end of the spring of the tipping peg will be clamped into an angled saw-cut.

Alternatively, one can also use two rubber rings to provide the needed tension. You can surely also use two small wooden arms that press on the shaft.

The two adjusting surfaces (#5) each get two long holes 20 mm from the top and bottom, plus a block (#7) glued on the outside with 5 mm overhang. They serve as contacts for the counterplates screwed to the feather clamps of the magnetic snappers, and as end points for feathering. The two magnetic snappers are now screwed evenly onto the adjusting surfaces, as can be seen in the diagram.

The holes for the #10 screws in the #1 middle part are bored only after the complete assembly of the device; then the exact height can be decided. For the small squares of the set screws, a small hollow must be made from the back; I also fixed the screws there with epoxy resin glue. Before that, the middle bar (#1) is attached with its rear edge even in the center between #2 and #3, and the #6 brace is screwed onto the middle of the back of the middle part.

Now we still need the two feather clamps, which are made of two softwood blocks and two metal clamps. I shortened the two metal clamps somewhat at the front and glued them with epoxy resin glue into the deepenings drilled out with a 4 mm drill.

When gluing, you should lay a strip of cardboard, its thickness at least equaling the feather's thickness, between the two pieces of wood, so that the feathers will later be held securely behind the quill. If the feathering is to be applied straight or only slightly angled, the feather clamps can remain so.

The longitudinal groove shown here in the clamp is suitable for featherings that are inclined more strongly to the right. The clamp is, in fact, still straight, but the pressure points behind the quill are turned. To produce this groove, put the blocks in a vise with cardboard between their surfaces. Then place a shaft diagonally over the middle and mark the two edges. If you have a small hollowing iron, you can cut the groove with it. Then an arrow shaft wrapped in sandpaper (80 grade) can be used to smooth the groove.
This is somewhat laborious and goes better with soft wood. For left-tilted feathering the groove has to be made the other way around.

Attaching the counterplates of the magnetic snappers to the feather clamps offers the chance to even out any unevenness in height and depth. By adjusting the adjusting surfaces in the long holes with a shaft in place and the feather clamps on, you can then set the desired angle and situation and fix them with the set screws and wing nuts. The shaft is turned by turning the notch holder; I have marked the setting with a bit of nail polish.

I hope I have not scared you away from building it yourself through this description, and I assure you that building the device is simpler than can be described in generally understandable words.
Surely you can also improve one detail or another, for example, a simple means of adjusting the relation between the notch and leading feather.

Cutting Feathers

Text: Volkmar Hübschmann; Photos: Volker Alles

From left to right:
- The unworked feather
- Beginning and end of the quill cut off
- Split feather
- Cut upper side of the feather

In principle, every feather is suitable for feathering arrows, as long as it is big and firm enough. The approximately ten outer swing feathers of a turkey or goose are especially good, but the other feathers need not be rejected. Farmers who keep fowls have large quantities of feathers as slaughtering debris.

Feathers of waterfowl are especially well suited, since they are strongly impregnated by nature. A tip at this point: To impregnate arrow feathers, duck rump fat, which one can buy in fishing shops as fly and line grease, is very useful.

To obtain feathers, inquiring about molting feathers at animal or bird parks or animal protection organizations can pay off.

Very dirty feathers should be cleaned only with lukewarm water. Do not use detergents at all, as they will wash out the natural impregnation. Stuck-together bristles or arrow feathers that have become messy in the rain can be freshened up over steam from water. After cleaning or steaming the feathers, dry them carefully.

Before one begins to work the feathers, they should be packed in airtight plastic bags (freezer bags) and left in the freezer for several days. Storing at temperatures below zero kills off any mites.

If one plans to keep feathers for a long time, they should also be packed in airtight plastic bags along with insect repellent. A large amount of feathers is best divided among several plastic bags, for if something goes wrong because of parasites, the whole supply of feathers is not ruined.

When one sees the prices of cut natural feathers of full length, one sees that building a feather-cutting device is worth doing.

Then one can experiment with all imaginable feathers.

- Electric drill
- Bracket for the drill
- Sanding drum

The dimensions stated here apply to a drill bracket in which the distance from the pillar surface to the middle of the chuck is 91 mm, and a drum with a diameter of 77 mm is used. If the drill bracket has a different distance from the pillar surface to the center of the chuck, and if the diameter of the sanding drum is different, the dimensions should be changed accordingly.

Metal Parts:
- 2 sheet-steel strips, 1.5 mm thick, 300 x 50 mm
- 1 hinge, 120 x 33 mm, with attachment screws
- 1 box latch with attachment screws
- 1 aluminum angle iron 3.0 mm thick, 40 x 40 mm, 500 mm long
- 6 small flathead screws to attach the two sheet-steel strips
- 4 lock screws M8 x 100 mm
- 4 underlaying plates
- 4 self-locking M8 nuts
- 2 table clamps for homemakers and household devices

Cutting list for 40 mm thick birch *Multiplex**:
- Baseplate 260 x 500 mm
- Pillar for drill, 50 x 280 mm
- Adjustable plate 1: 135 x 500 mm
- Adjustable plate 2: 75 x 500 mm
- Feather-holding plate 1: 90 x 400 mm
- Feather holding plate 2: 60 x 400 mm

* *Mutliplex* is a laminated material that I find better than massive wood, since it does not warp. Naturally, it does not have to be birch *Multiplex,* for other types are equally suitable, but the thickness of 40 mm is important.

1. Screw or glue the two sheet-steel strips to the middle of the pieces of the feather-holding apparatus.

2. Screw the hinge to one end of the feather holder and the box latch to the other end.

3. Screw and glue the pillar for the drill to the middle of the left side the left side of the baseplate.

4. Drill four holes (8 mm diameter) for the screws in the baseplate. Countersink the holes on the underside, so that the heads of the screws do not stick out beyond the plate, and glue the screws into the baseplate (with epoxy or PU mounting glue).

Hole for table clamp

5. Drill and file 8 mm holes in adjustable plates 1 and 2 and in the aluminum angle iron.

6. Oil all edges and the wooden surfaces (with hard oil) and wax (with parquet wax) or paint them (with boat paint). Sand the surfaces very smooth.

7. Make the holes for the table clamps.

8. Attach the bracket for the drill and set the surface of the sanding drum at a right angle to the baseplate.
Attach the sanding drum so that the lower edge of it comes as close as possible to the upper edge of the angle iron without touching it.

9. Set adjusting plate 1 so that the distance from the upper edge of the two sheet-steel strips to the sanding drum is about 1 mm.

10. Set adjusting plate 2 so that the feather holder can be slid play-free through the resulting groove.
The threading over the nuts should be sawed off for better handling.

11. Adjust the aluminum angle iron so that the sheet-steel strips come as close as possible to the sanding drum without touching it.

When the whole device is adjusted exactly, tighten all four nuts and fasten the device to the workbench with the table clamps. Now cutting the feathers can begin.

The work steps for cutting a feather

1. Fasten the blade of a cutting knife in a vise at a 45-degree angle.

2. Cut the quill of the feather in the middle, using both hands. A righthander pulls the quill onto the blade with the right hand and guides the cutting with the left hand.

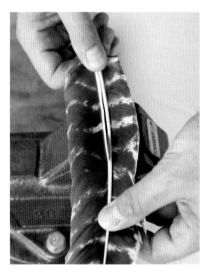

This process requires some practice and fingertip feeling, so that the cut does not depart from the middle.

Depending on the structure of the feather, both the upper and lower parts can sometimes be used for feathering. In a right-twisted feather, though, the lower part is twisted to the left, and the converse is true of a left-twisted feather, where the lower part twists to the right.

3. Clamp the split half of the feather into the feather holder.

Move it past the sanding drum in a vertical position, in order to reduce the quill to the desired thickness.

Move it past the sanding drum in a horizontal position to reduce the quill to the desired width.

Feather Burner

Volkmar Hübschmann

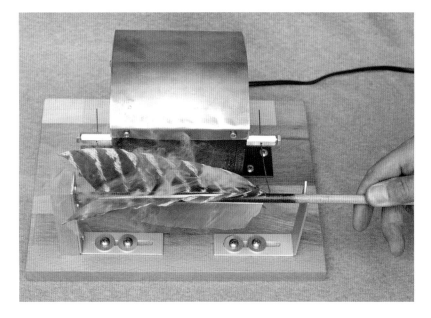

A feather burner is relatively easy to build. The principle is simple:
A wire connected to a power source and bent into the desired shape is raised to glowing heat by the electric current.

The arrow fitted with feathers cut only to length is put into a holder and the shaft is turned on its own axis. When turned, the feathers touch the glowing wire and the excess is singed off in exactly the shape of the wire.

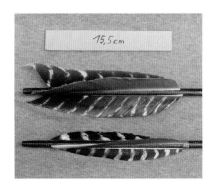

When the temperature of the wire matches the speed with which one turns the feather past it, the cutting angle—or the burning angle—is at least as exact as a stamped angle would be.
The brownish coloring on the singed edge of a white feather is especially visible, and if one strokes it several times, the coloring scarcely decreases.

It takes some experimenting to find a suitable wire and a suitable power source (transformer). How much power is needed depends on several factors:
• the metal (alloy) of which the wire is made
• the diameter of the wire
• the length of the wire
All of these factors together determine the resistance of the wire.

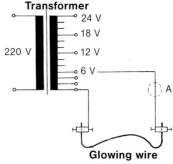

For orientation, here are the data for my feather burner:
• A chrome-nickel wire, 1.2 mm diameter, with a resistance of 6 Ohms per meter. This wire is used to build heating elements; it is a very tough material
        that keeps its shape without problems, even in a glowing state.
• To make a glowing wire for a certain feather shape, I begin with 40 cm of wire. The effective length of the wire (the glowing part) is about 30 cm long. Variations in the effective length of the glowing wire, determined by various feather lengths and shapes, of +/- 10 cm (starting with 30 cm of effective wire length) show no recognizable difference in the glowing behavior of the wire and thus have no effects.
• The transformer has a power of 180 VA/10 A, and varying tensions of 2-24 V/10 A can be subtracted. The transformer is set at 6 Volts. The mathematical result is a power strength of some 3.2 A with an effective wire length of some 30 cm.

When making the feather burner, one is relatively free; here are the dimensions of my design.
The baseplate is made of glued beech wood, 30 x 22 cm, 19 mm thick.
The housing is an open quadrilateral, open above and below, with outer dimensions of 13.0 cm width, 12.5 cm depth, 12.0 cm height, made of 9 mm thick birch multiplex, painted black. I deliberately used non-conducting materials.

Inside the housing is the transformer, screwed onto the baseplate. The two rear corners are strengthened with aluminum angle irons.
On the back of the housing are two holes, the lower one for the power cable, the upper one for the switch.

Drill a hole on each side of the housing, 8 cm up from the baseplate, and put an M6 x 20 hexagonal bolt through each hole from inside. The cables are to be attached to these bolts with ring cable shoes, which deliver the power to the glowing wire. They also serve to attach the M6 coil cases (the holders for the glowing wire) firmly to the housing (use two washers on each side, so as not to damage the housing).

Bore a 2 mm hole exactly in the middle of each hexagonal M6 coil cases.
The holes should be 16 cm from each other.
This distance determines the maximum feather length hat can be burned. Screw M6 x 15 hexagonal bolts into the outer ends of the coil cases to attach the glowing wire firmly to the cases.

The housing is attached to the baseplate by two angle irons. I made the top out of a curved piece of sheet brass.

The arrow lies on two right-angled aluminum brackets at a distance of 5 cm from the housing. If the holes are bored absolutely vertically in the coil cases, one can insert small nails in the holes, which makes the centers for the holes in the angle irons (V-channel, sack hole) easy to locate.

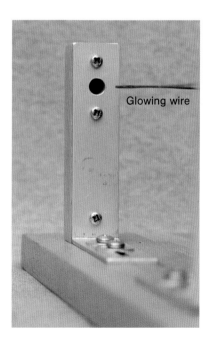

Glowing wire

In this way it is assured that the glowing wire is right in the middle before the shaft. The angle irons are screwed to the baseplate through long holes. The long holes allow an adjustment of the contact points. On the right angle iron, the arrow is held in a V-channel.

To the left angle iron there is also a 2-cm beechwood block screwed. Through the middle of the angle iron a sack hole 12 mm deep is bored (8.5 mm for 5/16" notches) into the wooden block. This hole holds the arrow notch when the shaft is turned for burning.

It is self-evident that the glowing wire is under tension only during the actual burning process.
When the feathers of an arrow are burned, the burner is turned off immediately until the next arrow is put in place. It takes only a few seconds for the glowing wire to become ready for use again.

The desired feather shape is at first drawn on stiff cardboard and cut out. The cardboard pattern can be shaped very well (with sandpaper).
When one is satisfied with the shape of the pattern, the shape is transformed to a piece of hardwood board about 5 mm thick.

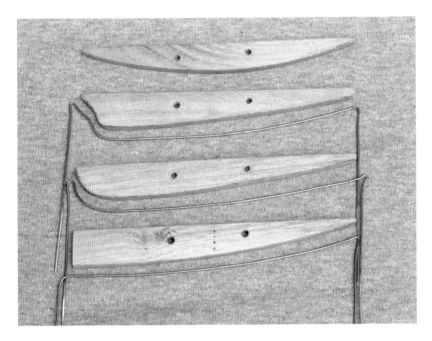

After the hardwood pattern is sawed out (jigsaw or bandsaw) and the contours have been sanded smooth, the wooden pattern can be screwed onto a board.

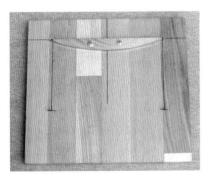

One can also make markings on the board to make the bending work easier.
At the places at which the ends of the quill are located in the finished feather, thin nails can be driven in as fixed points on which the wire can be bent sharply.

Using a small wooden rod, one can press the wire along the wooden pattern and bend it. It takes a little skill and practice until one has learned the bending characteristics of the wire; then it is very simple to form different burning wires. Sharp unwanted bends are almost impossible to remove and spoil the shape.

Naturally, the wire has to be adjusted in its final shape on the feather burner. To do this, lay an unfeathered shaft on the holders and check or correct the distance from the wire to the shaft. My tip: Better to buy a meter more of wire; then the first attempts can go wrong and one still has enough material to bend several perfect glowing wires.

De Luxe Feathering

Herbert Mueller

When I began with archery and still bought my arrows from a dealer as finished products, I read a sentence in his catalog that burned its way deep into my memory:
"A good arrow is the advertising sign of every archer," it said.
It also said that a good archer makes his own arrows.

A completely different reason for the kind of arrows that I make now was the fact that the bits of feathers left after stamping bothered me.
A five-inch feather can easily be cut out of a full-length feather, and the remainder is still long and good enough to be used.

To be able to make various color divisions on my spliced feathers reproducible, I used a simple graphic program to make patterns for the feather shapes that I use, and used a felt-tip pen to color designs showing in advance how I wanted to combine the feathers.

For the front part of the shaft I use a wax glaze with a teak color tone, for it enhances the grain of the wood nicely and gives the arrow a warm brown tone.

The rear part of my arrows is always colorful. After initial negative experiences with spray paint, I began to use only stains.
The look of a arrow—for the snow-free period—is always this: The last three to four inches of the arrow are always the same, namely white with a white notch.
It would surely not satisfy every archer, but I personally am of the opinion that the white stands out best in flight against the green and brown of the forest, and I can thus follow the arrow better.

I also always make the curve the same. For me as a right-handed archer, it is really immaterial whether it is a left- or right-handed spiral.
My eye follows the arrow better when the arrow rotates. The fact that it is slowed down minimally as a result I accept in the bargain, since I can see my arrow better. When the arrow rotates, the eye automatically concentrates on the movement and thus becomes more keenly aware of the flight.
The rest of the design is different for every set of arrows.

Materials
• a normal modeling knife with removable blades
• *Clipper-Vario-Stamps* with various forms for left- and right-handed arrows
• thin *Tesa* adhesive tape
• a rubber mallet
• a sharp soft pencil
• a hard base for cutting
• a ruler with inch and centimeter markings
• tweezers

Simple Feather Splicing

One starts with the rear end of the feather. Depending on how long the end is to be, the feather is laid in the groove of the stamp. So that no overly long piece, or the whole feather, hangs out of the stamp and makes combining the individual pieces difficult, I cut from a whole feather only as much as I need for splicing.

When I use right-handed feathers, I begin from the left; with left-handed feathers, from the right. In splicing it is important to make sure that the feathers show the same angle of the bristles and the quill is as nearly equally high and wide as possible.

The quill can be fitted afterward by smoothing or trimming to fit. If the bristle angle is not right, then I look for another piece of feather or cut a new piece from a fresh feather.

It is very important that the quill is cut through about in continuation of the bristle angle. This allows better positioning of the next piece of feather, and also gives the feather more of a hold when it is glued.

I have become accustomed to making about the last inch (2.5 cm) or even a little more white. The *Clipper* stamps have inch markings that make good application points.

If I just want to make a simple splice, I cut the front part of the feather on the quill at the same angle as the white back part. I change blades at the right time, so that it is always sharp and makes a neat, straight cut.

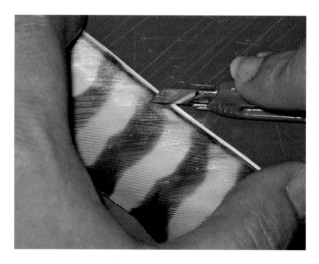

It will happen often that the quill proves to be a bit stubborn or very soft. Then one must hold the feather rigid with as many fingers of the other hand as possible and cut through the quill so that the cut runs at a right angle to the quill, but always in the direction of the bristles.

Of course, in the beginning not all cuts will be surgically perfect, but as the saying goes, practice makes perfect!

The cut-off piece of the feather is now laid in the groove of the stamp and se onto the white piece. The quills can also be placed together or overlapping in the groove.

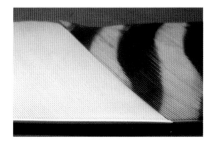

By cutting the quill at an angle, the quills of the feather pieces then overlap, even if the quills are not supposed to fit together absolutely perfectly.
The bristles of the two feather pieces are hooked together by running a finger over them.

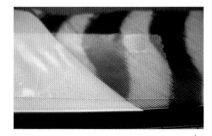

So that nothing more can slide out of place while stamping, the seam spot is secured with a streak of Tesa tape.
Interestingly, the strip of tape from a post office is a little thinner than the Tesa tape sold in hobby shops, which is why I always use the type from the post office.
In the stamping process itself, the strip of tape is absolutely no problem.

When closing the stamp, I hold the feather pieces in the groove firmly to secure them, so the quills do not bend and snap out of the groove.
If the stamping knife is then lying on the bristles, the knife holds the feather in the groove. The strip of tape stays where it is!

With the rubber mallet, give a medium-hard blow to the stamp.
With the strip of tape, the feather pieces are stamped like a normal feather and the two-colored but complete feather is lifted carefully out of the groove.

De Luxe Feathering

Should it stick a bit, I lift the feather quill carefully with the tip of the hobby knife and can thus remove the feather neatly from the stamp without loosening the bristles from the tape.

For safety's sake, I lay the feather on the side the tape is on and push both parts of the feather onto the tape again, so that it cannot loosen again.

Now the feather is finished and can be placed in the feather clamp of the feathering device very normally and glued onto the shaft.

Multiple Splicing

Often I make the lead feather a little different in color from the other two. Here in the picture, the last inch (measured at the quill) of all three feathers should be white; the lead feather should also have three equally big pieces in rainbow colors (in color-wheel order).

It looks better and more subdued when the first added stripe is red and the last is violet. The front piece of the lead feather should also be white. Thus here two feathers with a simple splice and one with an eightfold splice are needed. Such a rainbow arrow is really eye-catching and well worth the trouble.

First I make the two feathers with a simple splice as described. The last inch is white; this is also true of the lead feather. For this one, the rear piece is the first to be placed in the holding groove of the stamping plate, up to the desired marking.

Next the six colored pieces have to be cut.

146

So I take stamped pieces of feathers (naturally, new ones can also be used, but then they can no longer be used for normal feathers, because they are no longer long enough) in red, orange, yellow, green, blue and violet and measure a piece of each one with a length of 3/10 inch. That is roughly 7.5 millimeters.

With such an eightfold splice, it must be absolutely sure that the feather quills of all the pieces are equally high and wide. Otherwise the pieces of feather will not lie evenly on the shaft and will result in an uneven and unpleasant total appearance. In the event that the quill width simply will not fit, the feather should be placed in a clamp of the feathering device and carefully smoothed and fitted with a small sanding block.

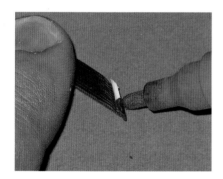

We begin with violet, the rearmost color. Then come the other colors in order; violet, blue, green, yellow, orange and red. Last of all comes a white feather piece.

Since I often make the strips of color that I have spliced into the feather run around the shaft, it looks better when there is no disturbing white quill showing between the colored bristles and the colored stripe on the shaft.

Before placing the piece in the stamp, I color the white area caused by fitting the quill to match the color of the feather.

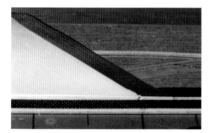

For this I prefer the paint sticks made by Edding from the 751 series, which have a point breadth of 1 to 2 mm.

By coloring it with paint, it looks as if the colored strips of the feather really wind around the shaft.

Every cut piece is carefully placed in the groove beside the last one, and the bristles are hung on. If that is too hard, one can do it with the tweezers.

Sometimes the bristles of two feather parts cannot be hooked together easily. Then I lift the forward piece a little with the knife and hook the bristles from the top.

This applies to right-handed feathers; for left-handed feathers it is done in the opposite way. When all six feather pieces are in place, the space at the front is filled with a white piece.

De Luxe Feathering

Over all the feather pieces I now place a strip of transparent tape. Thus all eight pieces are fixed so that they cannot slide when being stamped.

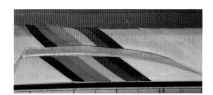

With a medium-hard stroke of the rubber mallet, the feather is now stamped. For such feathers, I most often and most preferably use the *Classic* shape. This looks in principle like the widespread *Shield* shape, but has a more highly arched back that gives a splice a better effect.

The whole thing is now carefully, or with a little help from the knife blade, taken out of the groove.

Laying it on the side with the tape, I press the feather pieces onto the tape again, so as not to lose any pieces.

These individual pieces held together by the tape can then be placed in the clamp and worked further like a one-part feather.

Splicing with multiple colored bristles

While splicing, it occurred to me that the two bright colors, white and yellow, do not form a good dividing line.

The thin yellow stripe consisted of five counter bristles; the rest of the feather behind it was white. Since I border the yellow stripe with two very thin black lines, I did not like the fact that these thin black lines did not continue in the feather.

So I decided to splice a single bristle into my next set of arrows, so that I could continue the two thin black dividing lines in the feather.

The back part of the feather is white again. Then I wanted to add a thin red stripe consisting of three bristles and framed by one black bristle on each side.

The front part consisted of a black and yellow striped feather.

For this feather division it is a good idea to make the shaft white from the back to the location of the red stripe. Ahead of that, a piece is stained yellow before the shaft takes on its warm brown tone.

The white piece of feather is laid in the groove of the stamping plate up to the desired marking. According to the feather shape, I leave the back part of the feather either one inch (3.5 cm) or 1.25 inches (3.2 cm) long.

148

Now the fine work begins, for now the blade of the model knife must be used to unhook a bristle.

To do this, I look for the place as near the point on the keel where the individual bristles are still visible and stiffest, and push the point of the knife blade carefully through between the bristle and the rest of the feather.

Then the bristle is pressed slightly to the outside until it has loosened from the other bristles.

Now the feather is placed with the quill on the firm cutting board, and the single bristle is separated according to the angle of the bristles.

So that the piece of quill that is needed for a usable gluing point at the bristle is not too small, I have often separated the foremost bristle from the quill first and only then cut the one that I wanted to stamp.

Thus the quill remains somewhat longer and can be laid better between the larger feather pieces.

Sometimes it happens that the quill turns slightly because the end of the bristle that is attached to the quill is very soft or thin. Then I make use of the tweezers to lay the piece of quill in the groove correctly. Likewise then the colored piece—in this case the three red bristles, and then another black one. After that, the rest is simple, because a good big piece of the striped feather is needed.

When all of the feather parts are lying neatly in the groove, they are all secured as before with a piece of Tesa tape, and then this feather can also be stamped.

Afterward, lift it carefully out of the groove, turn it on the other side and secure it by pressing all the parts again on the sticking surface of the tape strip.

Now this feather is also ready for further working.

Flu-Flu Arrows

Jürgen Knöll

There are various ways to feather a Flu-Flu, but the goal is always the same: the arrow should fly neatly and steadily for a short distance and then be braked very quickly so it does not fly too far.

This need arose from hunting: If one shot, for example, at a bird that sat on a tree branch, a normally feathered arrow would fly so far that one surely would not find it again in the woods.

In sport archery, a flu-Flu can also be helpful or downright necessary:
When targets are very close and the arrow could fly so far if it missed that it endangered others, or one would have to run a long way to find it again.

In high shots that go off clearly over 45 degrees, such as is the case in "Popinjay" (raven tree), a Flu-Flu can also provide very good service.
Here two types with different effects and efficiency are described. With all feathering it is important that the raw underside of the feather faces in the direction of the shot.
And a wrapping is advisable, as also for all other arrows, so that the feathers do not come loose and the archer is protected from injuries caused by loose feather quills.

One type is that of the arrow with multiple full-height featherings. These Flu-Flus are feathered four or six times with a feathering device or by hand. A twisted feathering increases the braking effect considerably.

The braking effect of such an arrow, compared to that of a "normal" arrow, is clear to see. To be sure, one can still shoot an arrow with sixfold feathering to distances of 70 meters and beyond.

Sixfold feathering can be attached easily with most of the feathering devices on the market. One puts the feather in as with a normal threefold feathering and glues the three feathers to the shaft.

When the feathering device is again in the starting position, one turns the shaft 180 degrees, puts it back in, and glues three more feathers on.

Flying Behavior

Shooting tests made with a glass-covered longbow of 50 pounds, and with a shot angle of 45 degrees, gave the following values with the various featherings:

- sixfold feathering   5-inch length, no twist   range 65 m
- single klob brush   full-length   range 40 m
- twofold klob brush   full-length   range 30 m
- fourfold klob brush   full-length   range 30 m

Simple Klob Brush

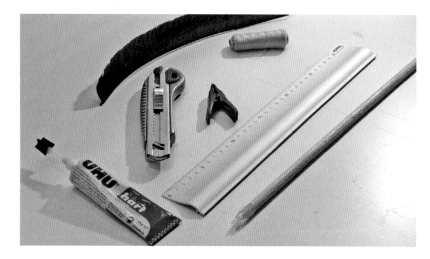

The second type is the so-called "Klob Brush".

As for this designation, one can surely say that it has arisen only in our day.

Here too, one can limit the maximum range of such an arrow to a certain extent by the number and length, plus height, of the feathers used.

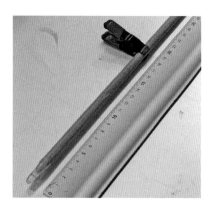

1. Determine the point at which the feathering is to start. At best, not more than the standing height of the bowstring.

2. Remove about 1 cm of the bristles at the beginning of the quill.

3. Glue about 1 cm of the feather on the arrow and attach it with the clamp. Let the glue dry (*Uhu Resin,* at least 20 minutes).

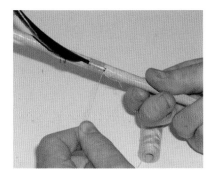

4. Remove the clamp and make a wrapping, to hold the feather better.

5. Brush the quill with glue (first read what happens afterward, for the following steps must go rather quickly).

6. Take the arrow between your knees or under an arm and the end of the feather in the left hand.
Be sure to hold the feather with sufficient tension.

7. Turn the shaft with the right hand and move with the feather in the direction of the notch. Be sure to make even spaces between the wrappings.

8. When you are 1 to 2 cm short of the notch, or when the feather ends, fix the end of the feather with a clothespin or another strong clamp.

9. Let the glue dry (*UHU Resin* at least 20 minutes, better an hour, since the feather is under strong tension).

10. Make a loop in the wrapping thread and pull this fast at the end of the feather before you release the clamp.

11. Shorten the feather quill to the desired length and remove the bristles at the place that is to be wrapped.

12. Apply the wrapping.

13. Now you can spread the bristles of the feathers.

Twofold Klob Brush

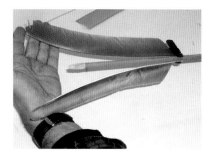

1. Select the spot where the feathering should start (at best not more than the standing height of the bowstring).

2. Remove about 1 cm of bristles from the beginning of the quill.

3. Glue the two feathers to the arrow 180 degrees apart for about 1 cm, and attach them with a clamp.

4. Let the glue dry (*UHU Resin* at least 20 minutes).

5. Remove the clamp and make a wrapping, to hold the feathers better.

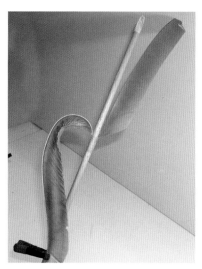

6. Bend the second feather away so that it does not disturb the first feather when wrapping.

7. Brush the quill of the first feather with glue (again, read first what happens next, for the following steps must go relatively fast).

8. Take the arrow between your knees or under an arm and hold the end of the feather in your left hand. Make sure you hold the feather with sufficient tension.

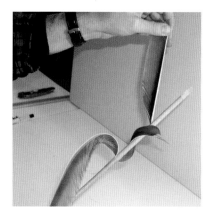

9. Turn the shaft with the right hand and move with the feather in the direction of the notch (when wrapping, be sure to maintain an even gap between the feather spirals).

10. When you are 1 to 2 cm short of the notch, or when the feather ends, fix the end of the feather with another strong clamp.

11. Let the glue dry (*UHU Resin* at least 20 minutes, better an hour).

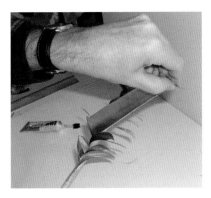

12. Now take the second feather and put glue on it.

13. Wrap it carefully in the spaces left by the first feather.

14. Make a loop in the wrapping thread and pull it tight on the end of the feather before you release the clamp.

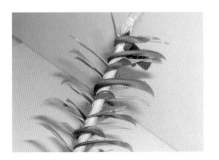

15. Let the glue dry again.

16. Shorten the feather quill to the desired length.

17. Remove the bristles at the place that is to be wrapped.

18. Apply the wrapping.

19. Now you can spread out the bristles of the feathers.

Tracers

Volkmar Hübschmann

Left with a tracer, right without.

In instinctive archery it is important that the archer can see the flight or trajectory of the arrow. Only so can the shot reach his subconscious mind, the basic prerequisite for instinctive shooting.

Being able to judge the targeting situation immediately after the shot is also very important, for whoever does not know exactly where his arrow is sticking can scarcely make corrections with the next shot.

Those archers who color the rear ends of their arrows as brightly as possible, use bright feathers (white is best) and bright plastic notches (even in glaring neon colors) usually have no trouble recognizing their arrows.

But whoever wants to stick close to historical original types, for esthetic reasons or to go with his equipment, and does not want to make his arrows so "modern", may have a problem recognizing his arrows under certain conditions.

I know from my own experience that recognizing an arrow that is red at the rear and is self-notched and feathered with dark, striped, natural turkey feathers, can be problematic.

Here a tracer provides help!

1. First cut, with a razor blade and a metal ruler, a neat straight line on the edge of a rabbit pelt.

2. Starting from this edge, cut strips of pelt two or three millimeters wide. Cut carefully, so that only the leather needs to be cut through; never cut the hairs along with it!

3. The strips of pelt can be trimmed to a length that represents the circumference of a shaft and glued to

Whoever has no white rabbit pelt can also use white down feathers.

The soft hairs of the pelt lay down during the arrow's flight, creating a small white point. The tracer increases air resistance only insignificantly, with scarcely any braking effect. When the arrow hits the target, the hairs stand up, making a relatively large white point that makes the arrow easy to see.

Bowstrings

Gallows for Flemish Plaited Strings

A Flemish Plaited String

Endless Strings

Central Wrapping and Nocking point

String Silencers

String Holders

String Wax

Gallows for Flemish Plaited Strings

Volkmar Hübschmann

Whoever masters the technique of bowstring production can plait a bowstring himself, for example, with the help of a long board with two nails driven into it.

Whoever wants to learn bowstring plaiting and values a precise, comfortable and reproducible work, and whoever makes bowstrings often, will find making a bowstring gallows of value.

In my design I have combined the advantage of the bowstring board and that of the gallows. The advantage of the board is the use of varying-length graduated fibers, that of the bowstring gallows is, as I see it, better handiwork.

The graduated lengths of the individual fibers automatically give a beautiful, evenly running splice. The lower splice is slightly shorter. This trick provides for two equally long splices, although the upper bowstring loop is made larger.

The bowstring gallows consists of two parts that are fastened together by screw clamps at a required distance. One can attach the upper and power parts to the edge of a long table or workbench.

In my case, a two-meter aluminum profile rail (50 x 20 mm) that I put in a vise has worked best. In designing the wooden part, one is relatively free, as only the intervals of the pegs and the rows of nails must be kept exactly.

My bowstring gallows consists of two hardwood boards (some 13 mm thick) glued together. In the upper board are the holes for the pegs (10 mm diameter). The holes for the screw clamps run through the middle of the gluing.

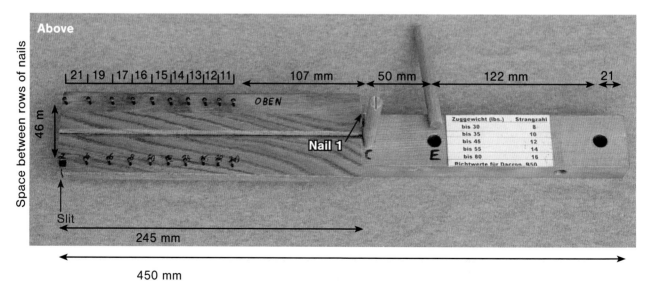

Peg C (80 mm, total length 93 mm)

Peg E (80 mm, total length 93 mm)

The C, D and F pegs are glued in, F is 2 cm shorter than D. Peg E is not glued in, so that it can be inserted in two different holes. All the pegs except F project 8 cm out of the glued board.

Right in conjunction with Pegs C and D, there is one small hardwood board each on the glued board with a 3 mm deep V-shaped channel glued on. The channel must be exactly in the flow with the pegs and right in the middle between the rows of nails. The channel serves as a guiding groove for the knife blade when one separates the bowstring cords.

Attention! Before driving in the 40 nails (2 mm diameter, 18 mm long), be sure to drill the hardwood board first, so the wood will not split. The nails should all project one centimeter out of the board. As shown in the illustration, cut a fine saw-cut about 2 mm deep at the upper edge of the board. Directly on the edge of the upper board, near Peg C, drive a nail (Nail!) into the glued board, and another nail 2 cm from the edge of the lower board, behind Peg D.

The two nails serve to set the length when reproducing a bowstring. The string loops of an already used and twisted bowstring are hung on the two nails, then the upper and lower parts of the string gallows are pushed apart until the string is stretched tightly, and fixed in this position. The new bowstring made with this setting is slightly shorter, since it will stretch to the desired length during shooting-in.
All measurements refer to the middles of the holes.

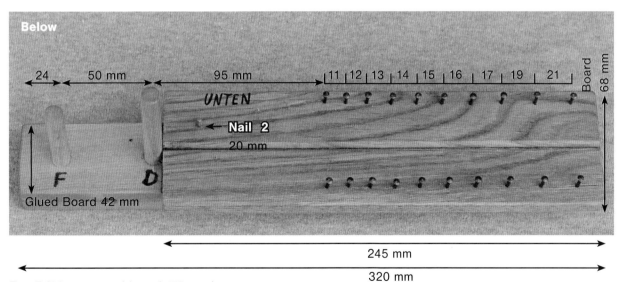

Peg F (60 mm, total length 73 mm)
Peg D (80 mm, total length 93 mm)

A Flemish Spliced Bowstring

Text: Volkmar Hübschmann; Photos: Volker Alles

I hope nobody will be held back by the very extensive introduction to bowstring plaiting. Many small actions are needed to produce a bowstring, and they must all be described—hence the extent. Once you have understood the basic principle of bowstring plaiting, it is really not hard. With some practice, the third or fourth bowstring will be almost perfect.

If a bowstring is already on hand and is to be reproduced, the length setting is made over Nails 1 and 2.

Without a model string, set up the string gallows so that the distance between Pegs C and D represents the desired string length. A new Dacron string stretched about 1.5 cm during shooting-in, so set the distance between the two pegs accordingly.

Materials
- Bowstring yarn
- Bowstring wax and small leather strip
- Middle wrapping (such as Brownell No. 4)
- Middle-wrapping device (it can be done without one, but such a device really makes the work easier)
- Unwaxed dental floss
- Fast-setting glue

Numbers of Cords—Pulling Weight for Dacron B 50
- 8 cords—to 30 lb.
- 10 cords—to 35 lb.
- 12 cords—to 45 lb.
- 14 cords—to 55 lb.
- 16 cords—to 80 lb.

The number of cords is determined by the pulling weight of the bow, depending on the archer's drawing length.
Whoever does not know how many pounds he actually has "at his fingertips" can find out with a pull scale and a measuring arrow.

Now it must be decided whether the bowstring is to have a spliced loop only at the top and be attached to the lower limb with a bow-builder's knot, or whether two loops should be spliced in.

Attention! In bowstring plaiting, one generally has to be careful that all the cords are pulled equally tight. This tension provides uniform stress on all the cords; no cord may hang loose in the strand.

1. Unwind some cord, knot the beginning of it, and hang the cord in the slit.

2. Variant A: For a bowstring with two loops:
Wrap the cord from the slit out, as in Sketch 1, around the nails until the desired number of cords is reached.

Sketch 1

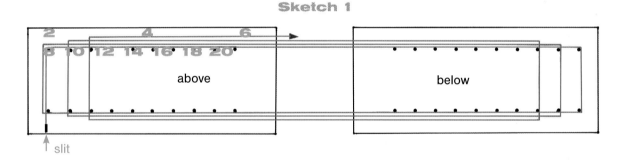

Sketch 2

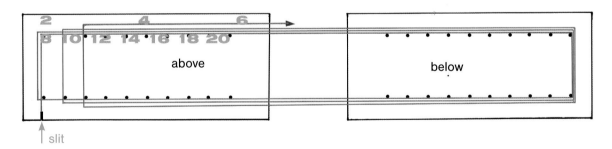

2. Variant B: For a bowstring with just one loop and a bow-builder's knot:
Wrap the cords around the nails from the slit out, as shown in Sketch 2, until the desired number of cords is reached.
The green numbers in the sketches show the numbers of cords.
The bowstring cord must be wrapped tightly around the nails!

3. With a knife run through the channel, separate the cords.

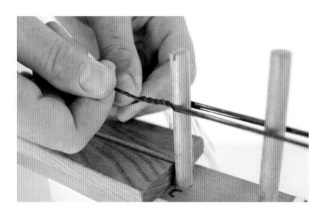

4. The Upper Loop

The two main strands are now crossed behind Peg C, turned clockwise and crossed counter-clockwise.

The number of crossings determines the length of the wound area behind Peg C.

The size of the bowstring loop is determined by the length of the wound area. Giving directions here is difficult, as the loop size must fit the tip or limb in question.

5. The wound area is now carefully removed from Peg C and placed around the peg to form a loop, which later forms the bowstring loop.

The two ends of the string are placed on the two main strands.

6. The two main strands of the string with the prepared, stepped ends are also wound again. In this phase one can check on the bow to see if the loop fits.

7. After the beginning of the splice is somewhat wound, the variable Peg E is placed in the hole before Peg C, and the already-wound area is secured with a clamp.

8. Now the lower end of the bowstring can be cut.

9. In order to "comb out" the two main strands, let the individual cords slide through your outspread fingers.

10. The beginning of the splice is now wound further until the stepped ends run out on the two main strands in the splice. The splice regularly becomes thinner.

When all the stepped cords are plaited into the splice, one adds a few turns. It is important when making a bowstring with two loops that one counts and makes note of the total number of twists that were needed for the splice.
Peg E is now inserted in the forward hole and the splice is secured with a clamp.

11. Whoever is making a **bowstring with just one loop (Variant B)** winds the lower end of the string to a length of about 12 cm and secures the end with a simple knot. These 12 cm are the area in which the bowstring is attached with a bow-builder's knot. Then continue from #15 of the directions.

A Flemish Spliced Bowstring

For a **bowstring with two loops (Variant A),** the following additional steps are necessary:

12. The two main strands are wound clockwise and crossed counterclockwise—but this time not so tightly and firmly as in a splice, but loosely over the length of the bowstring. The number of twists/crossings depends on the number of twists/crossings that were used for splicing the upper loop (see #10).

To be sure, increase the number of crossings by three. These twists/crossings will be used up in making the lower string loop.

13. The Lower Loop
Cross the two main strands behind Peg D and wind them. Plait one loop as described in #6. As a rule, the lower loop is smaller, since it stays in the notch when the bow is unstrung.

14. Hang the loop on Peg F and wind the splice (see #10).

15. The bowstring can now be taken off the gallows and twisted (about 50 twists, depending on its length). The height (the distance between the inside of the bow grip and the bowstring) is set provisionally by twisting and the bow is strung. With a folded leather scrap, one rubs along the bowstring to make it nice and round. In case the two strands do not want to blend into a smooth string but wind around

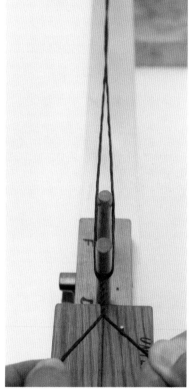

each other, secure both ends of the splice and comb the cords in between again. Then twist the string counterclockwise again and rub it smooth again.

16. So that the new bowstring reaches its final length, make about twenty shots and then adjust its distance exactly by twisting.
17. The whole bowstring is now ready to be rubbed with string wax. Don't forget the loops! The string wax is rubbed thoroughly into the string with the leather scrap. Strong rubbing produces heat, which makes the wax melt.
Check the distance again and correct it if necessary.

Endless Bowstring

Text: Ekkehard Hoehn; Photos: Volker Alles

In endless bowstrings, the strands lie parallel to the long axis of the string (only when the string is turned is a small angle created). For this reason they are somewhat less stretchable then Flemish spliced bowstrings.

Naturally, one can make endless bowstrings in slightly different ways. Here I'll show you my method, which has worked well for me.

Materials

- Modern bowstring yarn, *dacron* (polyester) or *Fast Flight (Spectra, Dyneema, Vectran)*.
- Yarn for wrapping the loops and the middle of the string.

There are three types of wrapping yarn:

A. Monofilament consists of a single thick nylon cord and can be used only for wrapping the middle. Monofilament is somewhat hard to work, as it is hard and smooth. If used for the loops, it can slowly but surely cut through the bow limb.

B. Twisted nylon consists of many thin, twisted nylon fibers and is well suited to wrapping the loops. If used on the middle, it will prove to be less durable.

C. Plaited nylon, which is very durable as a middle wrapping.

. Wrapping device for wrapping the loops and middle.

. A bowstring gallows in which the string is wrapped. You can buy it or build it yourself. In principle it is just four pins that are arranged, turnable and adjustable, in pairs on a tube rack. (If necessary, one can also improvise with a few screw clamps on a tabletop.)

. Cutting tool (knife or shears).

Step 1: Determining the length of the bowstring

First set the gallows in a vise to keep it firmly in place. Then set the four pins of the gallows in a line and stretch your old bowstring around the two outside pins. Adjust the pins to plus or minus the distance that the new bowstring should be shorter or longer.

In determining the bowstring length, you must consider:

If you are changing from a Flemish string to an endless one, your new endless string must be somewhat longer than your old Flemish one, since it stretches less when strung.

If you are changing from a dacron bowstring to a *Fast Flight,* the latter must be longer than the old dacron string because it stretches less.

Step 2: Winding the yarn around the pin

Tie the yarn loosely to one of the inner pins, so that some 30 cm of the yarn hangs loose, and then wrap it with even tension around the outer pin, always to the outside, half as often as your finished bow-string should be thick, thus eight times in a 16-cord bowstring.

After you have done the wrapping, leave another 30 cm of yarn hanging and then cut the yarn off.

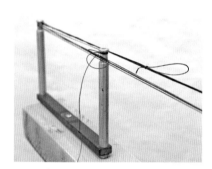

Step 3: Knotting the two yarn ends

The overhanging end of the yarn is led around the outer pin and tied with its bowstring.

To do this, wrap the yard end in spiral form around the bowstring and make a knot at the end. It does not matter how, as long as the end stays tight.

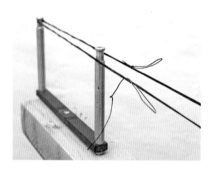

The beginning piece of yarn attached to the inner pin of the gallows is then loosened, led around the outer pin, and attached to the outer string strand in the same way.

The two yarn ends are one over the other about 20 cm out, and at this place (one of the later loops) the string is thus 17 strands thick,

ca. 25 cm

Step 4: Crossing the pin and applying the loop underwrapping

The gallows is loosened and the closed strand of the bowstring is taken off. Now set the pin of the gallows in a crosswise position and wrap the bowstring strand around the pin again.

The position of the bowstring strand between the two knots is then placed around both pins on one of the short sides of the gallows rectangle. Take the wrapping yarn with the wrapping device and first make a wrapping about 20 cm long between the pins (for the wrapping technique, see middle wrapping, below).

After that you can cut off the projecting (knotted till now) ends of the wrapping yarn, for the yarn is fixed so firmly by the wrapping that it can no longer slip.

Step 5: Setting the gallows pin to length and applying the loop overwrapping

The overwrapping closes the loops and thus makes a real bowstring out of two yarn strands.

To do this, set the gallows pin again according to length and place the string strand around the outer pin so that the loop wrapping is divided at both ends. When you position the string strand so that the ends of the underwrapping are not exactly opposite each other, but offset 5 to 10 mm, it provides a gentler transition to the overwrapping.

With the usual wrapping technique, apply the overwrapping to the loops.

Make sure that the loops have the right length for your bow.

Shortly before the end of the wrapping, make a loop 20 cm long of a piece of string yarn about 40 cm long. Then lay the loop on the string strand and overwrap it with a wrapping 1 to 2 cm long. Cut the wrapping yarn off the wrapping device and push it through the loop.

Endless Bowstring

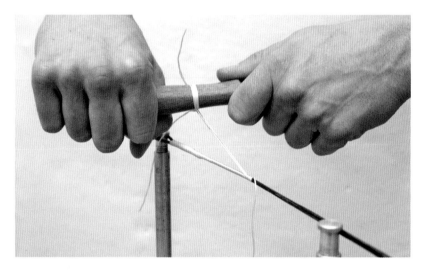

The yarn end is then pulled under the wrapping with the help of the loop and cut off.

For this you can wrap both cords of the loop around, for example, a hollow rod, so as not to cut into your skin, and you also have more power for pulling it through.

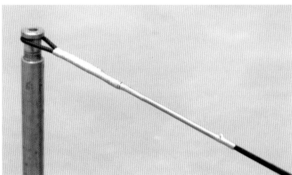

Step 6: Applying the middle wrapping
Make the middle wrapping long enough, but not needlessly long. With modern bowstring yarn you can make a very sturdy bowstring with a few strands.

It may be that your arrow notches are too wide for such a thin bowstring. To improve this (by making the bowstring thicker in the area of the middle wrapping), you can add a few pieces (some 30 cm long) of bowstring yarn to the wrapping.

Then string the bowstring on the bow and check the fistmele, Minor changes in the fistmele can be made by twisting the bowstring. An endless string should be twisted somewhat anyway, so that the individual strands will not relax (and cause a loss of speed).

Middle Wrapping and Nocking Point

Text: Volkmar Hübschmann; Photos: Volker Alles

Starting from the place where the nocking point will later be, the middle wrapping is applied beginning some 16 cm under the nocking point and extending some 5 cm above the nocking point. The beginning and end of the wrapping can be marked with, for example, a piece of knotted cord.

1. To start, the beginning of the yarn is conducted along the bowstring at the lower end of the wrapping and around the yarn, and laid on the bowstring. One holds the beginning of the yarn in one's hand. Then one begins to wrap the bowstring and the beginning of the yarn.

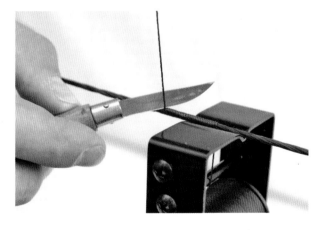

2. When the wrapping is about 2 cm long, one pulls again on the yarn, so that the loop is pulled very tight.
Then continue wrapping, and then the yarn can be cut off at the wrapping.

3. Finish the wrapping to about 1 cm before the end. The braking resistance on the wrapping device should be set so that the device hangs secure on the bowstring even while wrapping actively, but not so tightly that the bowstring is pulled in tightly.

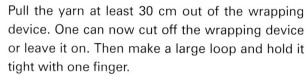

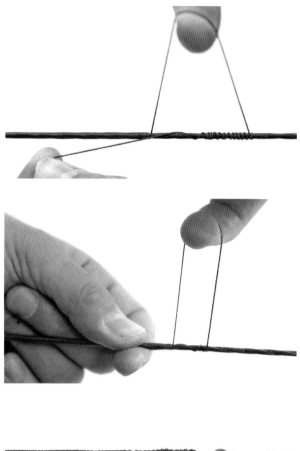

Pull the yarn at least 30 cm out of the wrapping device. One can now cut off the wrapping device or leave it on. Then make a large loop and hold it tight with one finger.

Beginning about 5 cm from the former end of the wrapping, make at least 15 wrappings in the same direction, but in the opposite wrapping direction to the previous wrapping.

4. Lay the yarn end on the already existing wrapping parallel to the bowstring and, keeping the big loop under tension, continue the wrapping. Thus the end of the yarn is wrapped over (same direction as the previous wrapping).

The previously made wrapping in the opposite direction will thus be used up.

5. When all the wrappings are used up, pull firmly on the end of the yarn, making the large loop smaller. So that the loop yarn does not make a knot, hold the loop under slight tension.

The yarn end that comes out from under the wrapping is pulled tight again and then cut off.

The Nocking Point

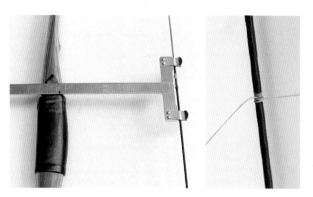

With a bowstring checker, determine the position of the nocking point.

At this point, a knotted wrapping of unwaxed floss is to be attached. With a drop of glue, the wrapped nocking point is secured.

If no glue is at hand, one can also wrap the nocking point with a thread of dacron and knot it, and (carefully!) melt it with a cigarette lighter.

Volkmar Hübschmann; Photos: Volker Alles

The sound of shooting a bow varies; recurve bows are often louder than longbows. Whoever is disturbed by this sound is brought help by bowstring silencers. Long-haired pelts, wool, rubber or dacron fibers are suitable for making silencers.

The unstrung bowstring is untwisted at the place chosen for the silencer, and the sound-damping material, such as a small bundle of wool fibers, is stuck through it. With the straightening of the bow-string, they are held fast there.

Trim them to the desired length. Wool and dacron fibers get worn away further through the use of the bowstring, forming almost spherical bundles. Dacron fibers should be washed with acetone in advance; thus the individual fibers will no longer stick to each other, and the silencer will become nice and fluffy.

Silencers made of animal hair take somewhat more work, but look very nice.
From a suitable pelt, cut leather strips about 20 cm long and 5 m wide (but with a knife from the skin side out), so that al the hairs run in the same direction perpendicular to the strip, and remove the hair from some 5 mm at each end.

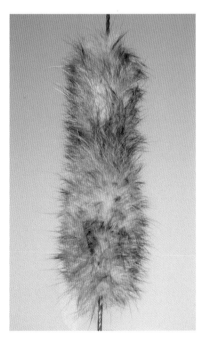

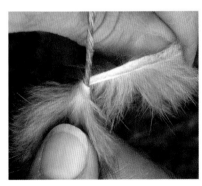

Untwist a new and thus only slightly twisted bowstring at one place and stick one end of the leather strip through it. The hairs then point downward. Then wrap the strip of pelt tightly up-ward in the direction of the twist in the bowstring, so that with every turn the hairs lie over the hairs of the previous wrapping.
At the end, stick the end of the leather strip back through the strands of the bowstring. The bowstring will now be twisted somewhat more tightly, which will hold the silencer more firmly in place.

Bowstring Holder

Volkmar Hübschmann

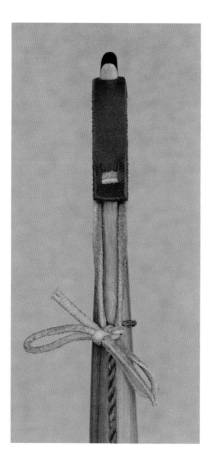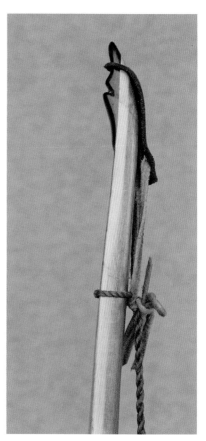

A bowstring holder holds the bowstring of an unstrung bow tightly enough so that the lower string loop cannot slide out of its notch. If one end of the bowstring can move freely, it will very probably untwist. In such a case the bowstring must be twisted again, so that the fistmele does not change. At worst, one might lose the bowstring while transporting the bow, if it should slide out of the notch.

A hole (1 cm in diameter) is stamped in the upper end of a leather strap (about 7.5 x 1.8 cm), then two parallel slits are cut in the power end. A leather belt (40-50 cm long) is threaded through these slits.

Turn the hole in the string holder over its upper tip, pass the two ends of the leather belt through below the bowstring tube, and tie them in a bow.

A bowstring is secured that quickly and simply.

Bowstring Wax

Volkmar Hübschmann

Bowstring wax sticks the individual fibers of a bowstring together, simplifying the plaiting of the bowstring.

But bowstring wax not only provides good service in the making of bowstrings; it also protects them from moisture and dirt during their later use.

When waxing a bowstring, one must not forget the loops, as it reduces the friction on the tips there.

Well-kept bowstrings last longer and are safer!

To make bowstring wax, one needs beeswax and some vegetable oil. With a little luck, one can get beeswax by the block from a beekeeper. But one can also use a candle made of rolled beeswax.

The wax is heated in a small pot until it is liquid. If particles of dirt should be floating in the liquid wax, they must be removed with a spoon. Next add a small squirt of vegetable oil to the liquid wax and stir it in.
The oil changes the consistency of the wax, making it smearier, so that it is easier to use and sticks to the bowstring better.
The liquid mixture of wax and oil should be put in a flat rectangular form to cool. The resulting wax bar can now be cut easily into long bars.

Rub the wax into the bowstring well, and rub over it strongly with a leather scrap. The rubbing creates warmth, which makes the wax melt, so that it can penetrate better into the bowstring.

Targets

A Simple Target standard

Animal Targets Made of Foam

Special Targets and Moving Targets

Target Standards Made of Locust Wood

Volkmar Hübschmann

Locust staves that prove to be useless for bow building after a trunk has been split do not need to end up being cut into small pieces and used as firewood. They are well suited for use as brackets for half a *Neopolene* plate.

Since locust is very resistant to rotting and decay, start by driving two unfinished, only pointed wooden posts into the ground (with a sledge hammer) some 70 cm apart.
Depending on the ground texture, the posts should be driven some 30-40 cm deep, so that they still project about 1.5 meters out of the ground.

Then nail a piece of wood about 1.20 meters long horizontally to the two vertical posts about 40 cm above the ground.

To brace the frame from the rear and serve as a base for the half-plate, two pointed pieces of wood should be laid on the crosspiece and driven in diagonally behind the panel.
It is good to set up the target in front of a low wall or mound of earth. The length of these posts depends on the conditions at the site; they should project forward some 20-25 cm.

On the forward ends of the projecting pieces, nail on a second crosspiece, about 1.20 meters long. The gap between it and the posts should be chosen so that the panel can easily be held in place.
To protect the panel from the weather, one can attach it to the upper ends of the vertical posts with

a piece of washline.
It is advisable to bore the holes for the larger carpenters' nails in advance; otherwise they will probably bend in this hard wood.

Animal Targets Made of Foam

Targets: Bernhard Hölzl; Text and Photos: Herbert Müller

Materials and Tools

- Vacuum cleaner
- Electric plane (or sander with coarse sandpaper)
- Hot-air blower, work gloves
- Regulated saber saw with extra-long saw blade for metal
- Two small sawhorses
- Water-insoluble thick felt markers
- Beamer, PC, better notebook
- Scanned animal pictures (such as from memory playing cards or catalogs)
- Long bread knife
- Carpet knife with removable blades
- Woodcutting tools, such as V-shaped blade for target lines
- Full and tinting paint (impervious to weather)
- Brushes of various sizes
- Flat plates, etc., for mixing paint
- Plates of *Ethafoam 400*

Who does not know them—the lovely and very realistic-looking 3-D animals from various makers. At many tournaments they are waiting to be shot. But not every club or bow department can afford all the targets for the competition in 3-D form.
In our club we are lucky that our groundskeeper is very creative in making targets out of sheets of foam. We have documented how he makes them to inspire you to make them.

According to our experience, *Ethafoam 400* sheets are the best choice for making targets. The material lasts much longer than *Ethafoam 200* and yet can be repaired easily.

Shot-up spots are simply cut out and replaced by setting fresh material in, or made sturdier by bracing on the back.
Since the painting of the animals on such targets always needs to be touched up and freshened up, it is no great problem if certain places on the target have to be replaced in this way.

Animal Targets Made of Foam

Before the work can actually be started, the surface of the plates has to be prepared.

The plates have a water-repellent layer on the surface that is caused by their production but would later make painting, and especially the adhesion of the paint, much more difficult.

Thus before working them, we plane the plates with a typical electric plane from the hardware store, until the gleaming layer is gone. This is done rather quickly and without much trouble.

When the plate is planed, we project the desired animal picture onto the prepared plate with the beamer. In the course of time, we have scanned many such pictures from animal pictures on memory playing cards, magazines or catalogs to serve as models.

Using the beamer gives up the possibility, sometimes by zooming the picture, to use the full extent of the plate. If the picture is projected sharply, contours, target zones and strong shadowings, etc. can be drawn on the plate with a waterproof felt-tip marker.

With a regular saber saw, set to a relatively slow speed and equipped with an extra-long blade for metal, the outer contours are cut out of the plate.

Because the metal saw blade has no coarse teeth and the saw is set at a slow speed, the foam does not get hot and thus does not stick fast to the saw blade.

The use of a saber saw is very kind to your shoulders; otherwise the contours would have to be cut out with a long sharp knife. The danger of the knife slipping is also avoided by using a saber saw.

If the animal picture, for example, has thin legs, then we leave enough material outside them for stability, so that the target will not weaken later. Contours can be cut into this border surface later.

An alternative would be to sticking scraps of foam on as grass, or painting them as a background.

At the same time, such surfaces have the advantage of catching arrows in case of near misses.

When all the contours and the spaces between, such as under the belly, are cut out, the material is doubled. Thus bigger scraps can be used. But it is important to make sure the cutting edges are straight, so that putting on and gluing another piece does not result in any cracks. It is a good idea to make sure the new edges are even with the former ones when you make the new layer.

Now the spaces between and the edges of both plates are warmed with the hot-air gun until small bubbles form on the surface. Then press the two sheets together with your hands and wait a short time until the material has cooled.

It is a good idea to wear work gloves, for the two plates usually cannot be pulled far enough apart so that the hands are far enough away from the mouth of the hot-air gun. Learn from experience!

At the start, a few gluing points suffice to attach the two plates on one side. That is important so that the plates do not slide, but still can be bent away from each other to be fully stuck together with the help of the hot-air gun.

Experience will tell you when the right time comes to stick the two sheets together. If you heat the material too much, it will melt rather like snow in your hand and create holes or low spots. The best time is when a slight formation of bubbles is seen on the surface.

Through heating and softening of the foam materials, they are properly joined when pressed together and will stand a lot.

With a retired bread knife, the edges of the front plate are cut, giving the second sheet the contours of the target.

Since there are unfortunately no saber-saw blades with a stroke of more than 10 cm (two plate thicknesses), each layer has to be cut individually.

It would naturally be simpler to glue the plates together first and then, in one step of the work, to cut the contours out of the ten-centimeter foam. At difficult spots, even with appropriately applied handcrafting ability, the saber saw can come in handy.

To strengthen the central area, a third layer made of scraps will be glued on, as described.
Three thicknesses of foam will even stop arrows from compound bows effectively enough so that they do not pass completely through the material and will not damage any feathers or fletches.

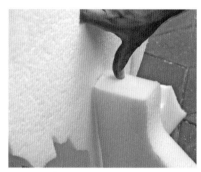

In the next step, at least one brace should be attached to the back. It is advisable to attach more than one brace to targets bigger than a badger or wild boar.
We make them similar to bookends, so that the pressure of an arrow's impact is directed to the rear.

Now it is time to cut the kill-line. With the carpet knife, a V-shaped groove is cut and the material removed.
An alternative would be the use of expensive woodcutting tools. They provide a finer line. When using the carpet knife, one should make sure that the line does not become too wide. So do not apply the knife flat when the groove is being cut.

To give the target a slight 3-D effect, the outer edges can be shaped with a bread or carpet knife. Some material is carefully taken off the edge with the blade, so that the target looks slightly three-dimensional.

One can attain more spatial depth by removing some of the surface from the space between the legs or on the edge of the body, where material was left for the sake of stability, so that the animals' body parts stand out more three-dimensionally.

In addition, when the target line is made, further contours and lines can be added to emphasize the body parts and masses.

Another possible way of creating spatial depth consists of gluing clumps of grass, stones, etc. made of foam scraps to the base. In principle, the same techniques or methods are used here as in wood or linoleum cutting. In places at which no material could be cut away, something can be added later in the painting, in order to simulate light and shadow.

Now the target has expanded so far that the painting can begin.

The most suitable paints are full and tinting colors for the inner and outer regions. Yet it is important that they be weather-resistant. Since they are water-soluble, they can be mixed without problems in painting, and so we can create any imaginable color tone. Any brands that are on the market are suitable.

Before the painting can begin, we must dampen the front of the foam well. It is sufficient to lay the target on the ground and sprinkle it with a watering can.

If a slight touch of a finger creates a small puddle around the fingertip, the material has absorbed its fill.

Sharply bordered color transitions can be painted only when the first color is thoroughly dry!

The watering makes it very clear that we have removed the outermost layer with the electric plane. Thus the water can absorb he water well and hold it in its pores.

This has the advantage that the paint itself does not have to be thinned too much and thus can penetrate more deeply into the pores when the paint is applied.

The water in the pores thins the paint applied with a brush and thus gives exactly the right consistency, so that the coat of paint lasts a long time and does not break off at once when an arrow hits it.

If the paint is thinned in advance and applied as a watery paint solution, the paint will not bond with the material sufficiently, because the too-thin paint runs right back out of the pores and scarcely covers.

It is recommended (as long as the possibility exists) that one work simultaneously on two or more targets, so that the paint on the other object can dry sufficiently. Usually the mixing of paint for smaller targets does not pay. Thus we always have two or more targets in progress, using more or less similar paint colors.

In the first work process, the main thing is creating the background for the subsequent color details. Sometimes this does not initially look just as it will at the end, but one should not lose patience right away if anything does not look right at the start. Simply let the coat of paint dry well and then paint the details over again or apply other colors.

The painting, of course, proceeds according to plan, but it is not lifeless painting by numbers or anything of the kind.
But after the first attempts, one quickly develops a good feeling for the colors, and soon the targets develop into little works of art.

The target must not be painted completely in one work process. It is better to put the paints away if necessary, in order to continue painting when one feels creative again. Corrections can always be made at a later date.
Just when a certain spatial effect is supposed to be achieved, it is always better when the lower layer of color has dried well, so that the often-necessary strokes of color do not run as a new coat. When the first coat has properly dried in its function as a covering coat, color can be pained onto color without previous watering.

The farther the process of painting goes, the more the plastic details are worked out by the application of paint.

Surely this calls for a little experience, but even in the first animal target, spatial and depth effects can be checked by placing the target at its planned distance to evaluate the appearance and effect.

Then the desired details can be improved or painted anew and checked again.

When the results are satisfactory, the work has been worthwhile and the archers will thank the creator often enough with their positive and admiring reactions.

A little extra work is called for when a target has been shot up thoroughly: We have observed that *Ethafoam 40* lasts a long time before it is so shot up that it flakes and the animal picture falls to pieces. As a rule it happens that the paint is more likely to break off and the animal must be painted again.

In a restoration, we usually reinforce the shot-up area—usually the kill zone—with another layer of foam and rework the paint of the target completely. Targets treated this way still have a good season ahead of them.

Special Targets and Moving Targets

Willi Müller

Special targets offer an unusual challenge. For example, it can be an extremely deep shot or an especially steep uphill shot.

The special feature can also be that the archer or the target moves. The situation becomes interesting when the shot at a first target effects the appearance of a second one, hitherto unseen. Here the archer's ability to react is put to the test.

Most of the time, special targets can only be achieved through the use of some technical design. In rare cases, though, the possibilities in a shooting range are good for a special shot, such as shooting through a root. Sooner or later, every range owner develops a sixth sense for such rarities and builds them into the course.

Many nice targets or shooting conditions are, unfortunately, not suitable for everyday use. Either they are far from the normal route, or the surroundings do not allow safe shooting.

Even though the challenge is so great in such cases, one should never forget the safety of the archer and his surroundings. An interesting shot without a safe range and background, with the danger of uncontrollable shots gone astray, or of breaking and losing arrows, should be avoided, even if it is hard to forego.

Special Targets and Moving Targets

In what follows, I would like to mention some special targets that are not based on natural circumstances, but rather can only be realized by technical means. These targets can be built anywhere as they stand or with variations.

General Requirements

- The design must be simple to build and operate.
- Every user must understand the design and operation at once and without instructions.
- The targets should also be usable by one archer alone. If additional personnel is required, the target soon loses its charm.
- The targets should be suitable for tournaments. It would be a shame if these attractions were kept from tournament participants. To be usable, shooting and replacing in their original positions should not take longer than shooting at a normal target. Special targets that slow down a tournament very quickly lose their attraction and become just an annoyance.
- Tournament suitability also means the same chance for all participants.
- Special targets should fit into the terrain or surroundings and be made of materials that suit the surroundings.
- A target with moving 3-D animals should be made as true to life as possible. As little of the technical aspects as possible should be visible. A target that turns—as I have seen—on an undisguised, terribly loud cement mixer is an unreasonable demand on any traditional archers.
- Special targets should be suitable for traditional archery and thus not be too technical. Motors, cables and batteries have no place in the field. Sooner or later they make a mess of the place. With imagination and new ideas, one can prepare for a shoot without these things.
- Special targets must be arrow-friendly. They should offer a safe catcher for the arrow. A target that turns uncontrollably or hangs absolutely free is not to be recommended for any length of time; the arrows sticking in the target soon become targets themselves and, since their whole length is turned toward the archer, are in danger of being ruined by shots. If they are free to move, they should be like mobiles that offer the archer several targets. Here a   change can be made to a new target after the first target has been hit one or more times. Thus the charm of the movement is not lost.

The Giant Pendulum

Design and Building: Markus von Rueden

As the first example of a moving target that meets most of the listed requirements, I would like to describe the giant pendulum. For years it has stood in our archery range; it is very popular and has never yet caused problems.

General Requirements

a) The pendulum may not be too fast.

Aimed shooting should be possible. If the pendulum moved too fast, good hits would be purely a matter of luck.

b) The swing time should be as long as possible.

If the pendulum soon stops, it must often be put back in motion. A long swing time means that there is an equal chance for several archers shooting in succession, since the swing time slows down very slowly.

c) The target should be very easy to change.

Every target becomes a bore in time. Changing the targets in number, shape and size can counteract this.

Materials

- Soft larch wood
- Beams
- Stramite sheet
- Screws, small parts
- Shredded wood balls

Use

Many shooting variations and challenges are possible with this target. Individual and group shooting can be done; shooting with or without a time limit is possible.

In the case of the Viking ship, many different scorings can be used, that offers challenges for good archers as well as successful experience for the less talented.

Design

- As a pendulum we chose a 5-meter beam with a cross-section of 10 x 10 cm; alternatively, a larch trunk can be used.
- The pendulum axis, an oak staff 20 mm in diameter, divides the pendulum in a 2:3 ratio.
- The pendulum axis is attached to the tripods with screw clamps.
- So that the pendulum swings as long as possible and not too fast, heavy weights must be used.
- To the shorter lower pendulum arm, a stable 50 x 50 cm board is attached.
- To this board a panel 60 cm in diameter and weighing some 40 kg is bolted.
- To give the pendulum nearly a balanced weight, with the 2:3 division of the pendulum, the weight on the longer upper arm can be considerably lighter, which makes assembly easier. The greater weight of the longer arm included, the counterweight must be only about 10 kg.
- With weights added to the lower arm, swing times and speeds can be influenced.

The rest of the design and the proportions can be seen in the photos. Thus I shall not include a description of the minutest details.
The panel that functions as a weight can also be used as a target. A round piece laid out as a field allows exact shot evaluation.

With a minimum expenditure of power, the target panel can be raised to its starting position about 180 cm high. When one lets it loose, it swings for about three minutes without having to be pushed again.

Other targets can be attached to the panel with long nails for a change.

The photo on the previous page shows a Viking ship made of *Ethafoam* 8 cm thick. The painted-on shields make very good targets and allow a stepped shot evaluation.

Behind the target, a wall made of 12 wood-shaving bales was built as a safe arrow-catcher.
To build and, above all, to erect a pendulum of this size requires at least four people.

Falling Grouse Targets

Of course one can also choose other types of targets.

Several archers can and should shoot at this setup simultaneously. Only then is it really fun.

Design

The grouse figures, cut out of reliable foam sheets and painted, are stuck up on round rods (broomsticks). With screw clamps the broomsticks are screwed horizontally on vertical pieces of tree trunks 90 cm long (if possible, larch about 40 cm in diameter), anchored in the ground. The holes in the grouse are made so narrow that the targets will not tip over by themselves, but only after a solid hit in their upper regions.

After some time the holes get worn, and new ones have to be bored. If this is no longer possible, the target has to be replaced. Shot-up broomsticks are also easy to replace.

Materials
- Five pieces of tree trunks
- 3 square meters of foam
- 4 broomsticks
- Small parts

Use

Many shooting and playing variations could be used on this target. It is especially interesting when several archers shoot at the same time. At the very last moment, many a grouse will be shot away before your nose.
If one wants to be successful, hast, precise shooting is called for. Bales of wood shavings are again to be recommended to catch arrows.

For tournament use, the following scoring can be recommended:

Kill zones, perhaps the golden beaks—for example, 20 points.
Body hits (only the front and edge count)—for example, 10 points.

Evaluation
Every hit counts, with a maximum of 80 attainable points.

Procedure
The archers of a group stand side by side in a row before the target.
All the archers in the group can shoot simultaneously on command. Each archer decides for himself which target to shoot at.
The shooting is finished when either all the arrows have been shot or no more targets remain to be shot at.

The charm of this target
One will probably do better to shoot slowly but carefully.
But it may also be that a faster shooter comes before you and shoots the target down. Fast shooting may detract from your precision.
Then too, after several hits, depending on the position or tipping of the target, the target surface can become smaller and smaller or no longer be visible.

Exciting shooting with chances for all, but many possible surprises, challenges to the tactical skill and ability of every archer, with new circumstances arising quickly. A real highlight of every tournament, and it is not only the children who enjoy it.

Flying Eagle

A special target is a simple design that can be set up in practically any shooting range. This is an eagle that moves in the wind at a variable height. Any other object suitable for shooting at can be chosen.

The higher the target, the more impressive and interesting is the shooting.

Design

A tree standing free on two sides, with freely projecting strong branches, if possible, and plenty of space in back, forms the spatial prerequisite. One finds these at the edges of open spaces, at the edges of woods, or along roads.

Since normally no ladder is long enough to make the needed attachments that high up, other ways have to be found. Here one asks an archer for help!

To make an attachment for the target as high up as possible, we shoot an arrow with a thin, strong cord tied to it over a projecting strong branch.

So that this succeeds and the cord comes back to earth after flying over the branch, a very heavy arrow has to be used. A fish arrow of massive fiberglass, or several arrows bound together, would be well suited.

One end of the cord is tied firmly to the arrow ahead of the feathers. The cord must be at least twice as long as the height of the branch over which one wants to shoot. Here it is easy to make a wrong estimate, so measure the cord very generously.

The coil of cord is placed on the ground, wrapped around an iron stake, by the archer, so that it will not slide off but can unwrap as smoothly as possible. Sometimes it is also necessary to unwrap the cord completely before the shot and lay it in slings on the ground, so that it can unfold easily. In any case, the free end has to be fastened to the ground.

Several attempts will surely be necessary before the arrow with the cord has crossed a branch at the desired height and landed on the ground. Here patience, skill and endurance are needed. But it is rewarding!

By the thin cord, the thicker, non-tearing or –weathering carrier cord (blue in the drawing) is pulled over the branch. We must use the thinner cord because we never would succeed in shooting a sufficiently thick carrier cord directly over the branch.

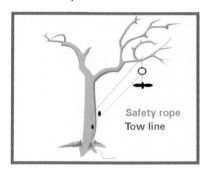

Safety rope
Tow line

When the thicker cord is pulled over the branch, the thinner cord can be removed.

To one end of the heavy cord, attach a heavy ring eye at least 5 cm in diameter. A roller is not recommended, as it will jam here sooner or later.

Through the ring eye, a second strong, weather-resistant cord, the pulling cord, is drawn. On this cord (red in the drawing) the target will hang later, and will be pulled up and let down.

The ring eye, along with the pulling cord passing through it, is now pulled up. The ends of the pulling cord must be fastened to the ground or held onto.

When the ring eye with the pulling cord has reached the desired height, the end of the cord by which it was pulled is tied firmly to the tree.

Now both ends of the pulling cord are hanging down from where the cord passes through the ring eye. The eagle is fastened to one end, and can be pulled up by the other end. After it reached the desired height, the cord is attached to the tree so that the target cannot fall down.

Without ever having to climb the tree, we have installed an air target that can be pulled upward almost friction-free and let down to remove the arrows.

In Brief

- Shoot the light cord over a branch.
- Pull up a heavier cord tied to this cord.
- Fasten a ring eye to one end.
- Pass the pulling cord through the ring eye and attach both ends of it to the ground.
- Pull the ring eye with the pulling cord upward.
- Tie the free end of the carrier cord to the tree.
- Fasten the target to one end of the pulling cord.
- Pull the target up.
- Tie the end of the pulling cord to the tree.

Materials

- One roll of strong parcel cord
- Two rolls of all-weather plastic cord
- One ring eye
- One foam sheet for the target
- Various small parts

Shooting

Extremely high steep shots are rare and very impressive. They can be varied by targets of various sizes, at various heights or greater distances from the archer to the target.

To fire at the target, Flu-Flu arrows should be used for safety's sake.

Shooting Barriers Open

This target is in the category of special targets in which a resting target is shot at. Hitting it releases a previously unexpected reaction. This reaction can, fo , consist of making a new target pop up or, as in this case, opening a previously blocked way.

Design

A barrier such as is seen at railroad crossings is built. The design can be seen in the pictures. The size depends on the particular location and naturally the path that is to be closed. The barrier shown in the pictures is located at the end of a small bridge that crosses the Glinde Brook on the Marsberg shooting range.

The counterweight on one end of the barrier beam is chosen so that the barrier, which is not held at the other end, will slowly rise up and be opened.

When the barrier is ready, a device must be built that holds the barrier beam down. In our case it consists of three angled wooden blocks to which angle irons are screwed that reach over the barrier beam.

When the blocks are knocked away, the barrier is unbolted and opens. Knocking the blocks away is to be done by shooting arrows. Since we can logically not shoot directly at the blocks, we must attach suitable target surfaces to them.

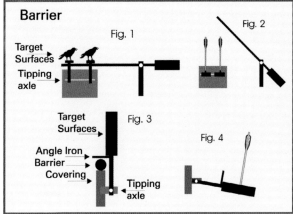

Barrier

Fig. 1

Target
Surfaces

Tipping
axle

Fig. 2

Target
Surfaces

Fig. 3

Angle Iron
Barrier
Covering

Tipping
axle

Fig. 4

Variations

The technical principle of a rocker used with this target can be varied in many ways. For example, instead of a barrier, the form of a fishing pole can be used, with a line hanging in the water. When the bolts are shot away, the rod rises up and pulls a fish out of the water, which can be shot at in turn. With imaginative but often minor changes and additions, birds can fly away upward, animals pulled out of the bushes, or coverings be removed. Tipping barriers and bolt designs can be concealed so that the archer cannot see the reactions.

Shooting

The barrier has proved itself in daily use and also as a tournament target. Although the effect is predictable, it always offers a pleasant surprise to every archer when he succeeds in shooting the way open. After crossing the bridge, one can set up the target for the next archer in a manner of seconds.

To be suitable for a tournament, a target surface must be present for every member of a group. One does not want to have to close the barrier again and set up the bolt after every shot.

One possibility consists of using as many bolts as there are archers in a group. Since this is often not possible for lack of space, you can get by with fewer bolts.

Then an additional, equally large replacement target must be installed, for instance, next to the barrier, for the archers who do not get past the barrier. On the range in Marsberg there stands a shield next to the barrier, which must be used as a target.

Materials and Costs

• Wood: Scraps, often free
• mall parts, such as rods, angle irons, screws, scraps of foam for targets, at minimal costs.

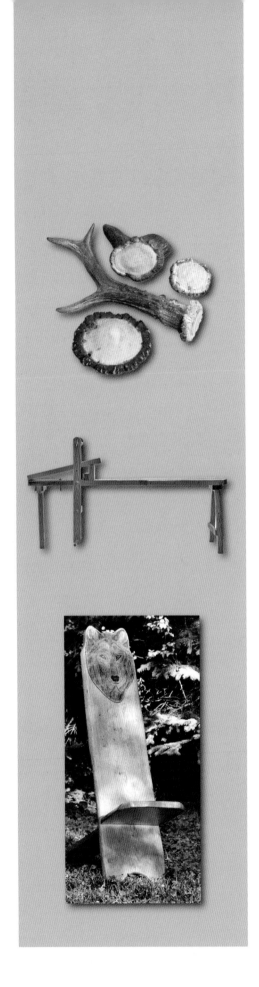

Other

Horn, Antler and Bone

Workbench

Shooting Chair

Horn, Antler and Bone

Volkmar Hübschmann

1.	Red deer throwing stick
2.	Red deer antler rosette
3.	Stag throwing stick
4.	Reindeer antler
5.	Roe deer shedding
6-8.	Polished cattle horn
9.	Unpolished cattle horn
10.	Plate of cattle horn
11.	Plate of water buffalo horn
12.	Unbleached cattle bone
13-17	Bleached cattle bone
18.	Bison rib
19.	Rawhide

Tips for Working

Horn, antler and bone can be cut well with an iron saw and shaped with a rasp, file or sandpaper.

To glue them, two-component epoxy resin glue works very well. An optimal gluing effect is attained when the glued surfaces are sanded lightly, wiped with acetone and thus degreased.

To polish the surfaces, it is best to use very fine (000) steel wool.

Bone and horn can be sealed with hart oil and parquet wax, which are also used on wood surfaces. Whoever has the handcrafting skill can also engrave the materials (scrimshaw).

With these three materials, one can make a whole series of objects that are interesting for traditional archery. For example, knife handles, handles in general, buttons and clubs, arrowheads, reinforced self-nocks, arrow plates, tip overlays, thumb rings, jewelry and decorations.

  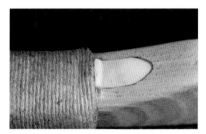

Small three-finger knife, blade of *Helle,* handle of bone, pear wood and horn.

Locust-wood bow with arrow

plate made of bone.

Horn

Horn is a hard albumen material containing keratin, formed by outer skin cells.
Claws, hooves, bills, nails, feathers, hairs and horns are made of it.
One can saw the massive points from cattle horns that were detached from bones and are clean inside. A tapering horn tube is left over. The tube can be sawn lengthwise and cooked slightly in water to make horn plates.

The soft horn can then be pressed into shape (for plates). Horn grows in layers, very much like the annual rings of a tree trunk.
If it dries out too much, it sometimes cracks along these rings. Objects made of horn should thus be treated with parquet wax from time to time.
The wax is a perfect protection and prevents the horn from becoming brittle or cracked.

Horn, Antler and bone

Antler

Antler is a branched bony growth from the forehead bone. It is dropped (shed) annually and grown anew by, for example, deer and reindeer.

Nice buttons and plates for decoration can be made of antler rosettes.

The antler roses look especially nice when their inner surfaces are ground and polished.

When working pieces of antler, the porous inner part of the antler in particular requires special care, as it is less stable. Whoever wants to make a massive knife handle with an appropriate diameter should remove it completely.

To make up for the removed mass, the antler tube should be degreased inside with acetone and filled with epoxy resin glue or two-component body putty from auto supplies.

Bone

Bone consists of calcium phosphate and carbonate, and has marrow and spongy tissue inside. In comparison with antler, horn and bone require somewhat more preparation before one can work them.

The cattle bones that one gets from the butcher can be sawn lengthwise and then cooked for about an hour. After cooking, the marrow and any remaining bits of flesh are removed.

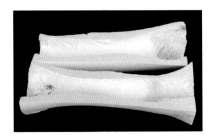

To make the bone relatively fat-free, it is then placed in boiling water with detergent. If one wants nice white bones, one puts them in hot water with oxygen bleach (laundry bleach) for a time.

The outlines of the desired shape can then be drawn on the dried bone and cut out with, for example, a bandsaw.

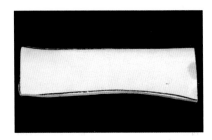

Bones are easy to get from the butcher. Horn and antler are harder to get. Inquiries at animal parks, with foresters and naturally with hunters for antlers or sheddings can pay off.

At flea markets, and even from recycled matter, one may find them. Whoever goes through life with open eyes can put together a useful collection of suitable materials.

Building Your Own Workbench

Volkmar Hübschmann

A workbench is a very practical and comfortable structure for clamping pieces of wood that are being worked.

It offers good service not only for bow building, but used to be part of the basic equipment of every farm, for tool handles and staffs, leatherwork and the like can be made on it.

My workbench is made of locust boards. Locust is a very firm and lasting, weather resistant wood, which is why it is also used for garden furniture, and is thus ideal for my uses. Oak, beech, ash and the like, the common native hardwoods, are definitely well suited as well. The dry boards should still have a thickness of 40 mm after planing.

The bench has a seta height of 55 cm and is 1.6 meters long. With these dimensions, the bench is also suitable for larger people. For example, one can easily clamp on a raw piece of bow wood and work it.

The special feature of my design in the possibility of inserting the axle of the rocker. The axle can be inserted in either the seat bench or the layout board. The axle through the seat has proved to be more favorable for working on a raw bow; the axle through the layout board is more suitable for working on smaller, uniformly shaped pieces because of the greater planing effect.

By moving the rocker axle, moving the wedge, moving the axle (five holes are available) and turning the rectangular clamp piece, there result a number of possible ways to adapt the height of the piece of work.

Since very few who are interested in making a workbench will have the chance to have the needed pieces measured and cut professionally, it is advisable to go to the carpenter with a list of pieces to be cut.

Rocker: Side View

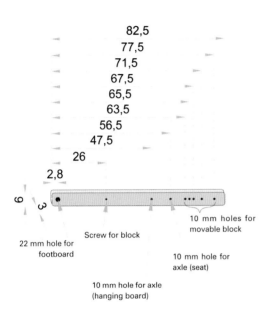

82,5
77,5
71,5
67,5
65,5
63,5
56,5
47,5
26
2,8
6
3

Screw for block

22 mm hole for footboard

10 mm holes for movable block

10 mm hole for axle (seat)

10 mm hole for axle (hanging board)

Rocker

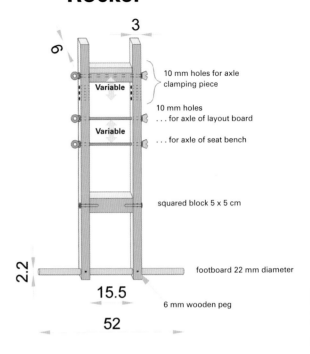

3
6

10 mm holes for axle clamping piece

Variable

10 mm holes . . . for axle of layout board

Variable

. . . for axle of seat bench

squared block 5 x 5 cm

footboard 22 mm diameter

2.2

15.5

6 mm wooden peg

52

(c) N. Hobohm 2004

(c) N. Hobohm 2004

The holes for the side pieces of the rocker must be absolutely right-angled and equal (make them together with a drill press), and the holes for the axle through the seat, layout board and clamp block must also be bored at right angles.

The assembly of the individual parts can be seen in the CAD graphics; first assemble the bench, then mount the layout board and rocker.

On the axles of the rocker and clamp, a wing nut should be glued with epoxy at one end.

The axle of the clamp block is screwed fast with a wing nut on the other side, the axle of the rocker is pulled on lightly with a hexagonal nut and then countered against the wing nut.
Use four washers per axle. Before the final assembly, all edges should be broken.

Clamp Block

15,5
4,5
5,5

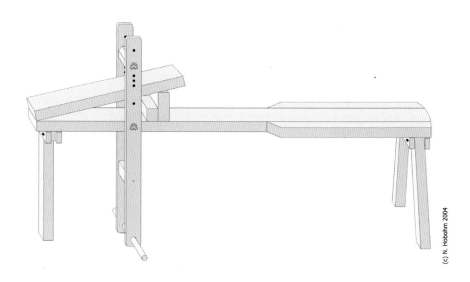

Wedge

12 mm wooden peg

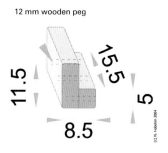

11.5   15.5   5   8.5

Seat

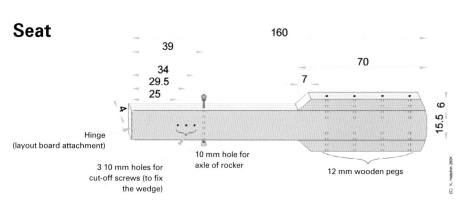

160

39
34
29.5
25

70

7

4

15.5   6

Hinge
(layout board attachment)

3 10 mm holes for
cut-off screws (to fix
the wedge)

10 mm hole for
axle of rocker

12 mm wooden pegs

Layout Board

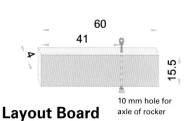

60
41
4

15.5

10 mm hole for
axle of rocker

Front Leg

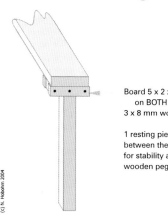

Board 5 x 2 x 15.5 glued
on BOTH sides
3 x 8 mm wooden pegs

1 resting piece of leg each
between the boards for
for stability and
wooden peg as buttress

Back Legs

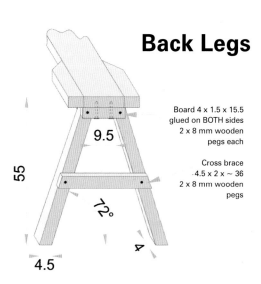

Board 4 x 1.5 x 15.5
glued on BOTH sides
2 x 8 mm wooden
pegs each

Cross brace
4.5 x 2 x ~ 36
2 x 8 mm wooden
pegs

9.5

55

72°

4.5

4

In the seat area, some 15 cm before the widening, all the edges are rounded, for your upper thighs are in this area when you work. Whoever decides to give his bench a nice finish—which I recommend—should treat all surfaces without exception, so that the wood, if it absorbs or exudes moisture, does so evenly. Uneven absorbing or exuding of moisture could lead to tension and cracking of the wood.

Whoever would like to can cover two more sides of the clamp block and the first 20 cm or so of the layout board with leather to guard against possible dents in the work and makes the whole thing less likely to slip.

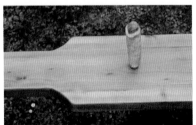

When working with the workbench, when the axle of the rocker is placed in the layout board it makes, in my case, an unpleasant angle for the legs. As a result of this bad angle, one's posterior slides backward on the bench and is thus scarcely in a position to put the right pressure on the footplate.

To help, I have built the "attachment" that prevents sliding. One bores a conical hole in the middle of the seat board, into which a brace some 25 cm long and padded with leather is inserted. The brace is likewise conically pointed on its underside the fit the hole. The place for the conical hole depends on the user's body size; in my case it is some 45 cm from the rear end of the board.

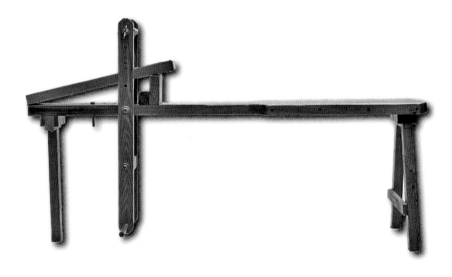

Materials and Dimensions

Wooden Parts		all dimensions in cm	
Seat	(1x)	160 x 15.5 x 4	seat board
	(2x)	70 x 6 x 4	wideners
Layout board	(1x)	60 x 15.5 x 4	
Wedge	(1x)	11.5 x 15.5 x 4	
	(1x)	5 x 15.5 x 4	
Front leg	(1x)	6 x 3.5 x 51	leg
	(2x)	4.75 x 3.5 x 5	
	(2x)	5 x 2 x 15.5	
Back Legs	(2x)	4.5 x 4 x 54	leave a bit longer, shorten after assembly
	(1x)	9.5 x 5 x 4	saw it in trapezoidal form
	(2x)	4 x 1.5 x 15.5	
	(1x)	4.5 x 2 x ca. 36	crosspiece
Rocker	(2x)	82.5 x 6 x 3	side arms
	(1x)	5 x 5 x 15.5	edge piece
	(1x)	4.5 x 5.5 x 15.5	clamp edge piece
	(1x)	52 x 2.2	foot rest (round wood) 1 wooden peg each, 6 mm, 8 mm and 12 mm

Metal Parts	(1x)	Hinge 10 cm 5 5 cm plus screws	
		Hexagonal wood screws:	
	(4x)	8 x 80 plus 4 U-plates	leg front/back
	(2x)	8 x 60 plus 2 U-plates	edge piece
	(1x)	Hexagon M 10 x 100	bolt to hold wedge. Cut off thread, file edges of the hexagonal head round
	(2x)	Threaded shank M 10	ca. 26 cm
	(8x)	Washers M 10	(outer diameter ca. 30 mm)
	(3x)	Wing nuts M 10	
	(2x)	Hexagonal nuts M 10	

Other   Watertight wood glue, epoxy glue, hart oil and parquet
floor wax or paint to finish the surfaces

Shooting Chair

Volkmar Hübschmann

A shooting chair, also called a trapper's chair, is easy to transport, quick to build, stable and comfortable.

I built mine of locust boards about 30 mm thick. With less stable woods or softwoods, I recommend using thicker boards. The upper end of the back is cut out in the form of a wolf's head.

The wolf's head is tooled on leather, which is glued to the wood and fastened all around with decorative nails.
The tooling was done by Joey Frosch.

All dimensions in cm

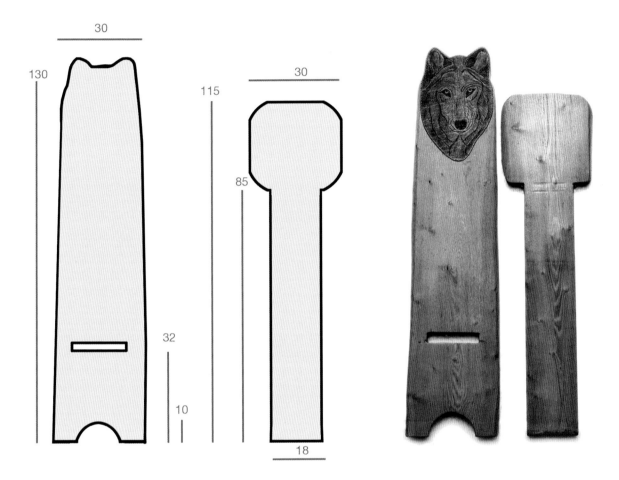

The stated dimensions offer only a general idea; one can form the desired angle of the chair and a comfortable seat height according to the height of the slit and the length of the rear "leg".

A good fit of the two pieces is also important. So cut the slit as precisely as you can; otherwise the back will lean too far back.

One can give free rein to his creativity in the formation.

All surfaces of the chair should be treated with a good finish (multiple oiling and waxing, or painting).

The parts of the chair that directly contact the ground can also be sealed with boat paint. With such treatment, the wood is scarcely affected by the weather outdoors or even a shower of rain.

The Authors and Artisans

Volkmar Hübschmann

Born 1961, trained photographer, was already interested in archery as a child and youth.

"From a massive fiberglass bow through a modern recurve bow to a compound, I have tried everything. At the beginning of the nineties I came into contact with the traditional archery scene. A short time later my interest in the wooden bow was awakened, and I began to learn bowmaking over the years by teaching myself.

"Working with other natural materials such as leather, bone and antler fascinates me just as much. Making a complete outfit for archery myself goes without saying for me. For only with self-made equipment can I develop my very own ideas and individual ideas."

Volker Alles

Born 1962, photographer and editor-in-chief of the magazine "Traditionell Bogenschiessen", archer since 1984, Kyudo (Japanese archery) since 2005.
"With great respect for the accomplishments of our ancestors I try to bring to life and maintain a small part of it for myself and all of us."

Joey Frosch

Born 1961, an enthusiastic Western hobbyist and archer. With his company, Betatakin, he runs a workshop in Mannheim and a business in leatherwork and Western equipment.

Uwe Gangnus

44 years old, has a theology degree and is a two-wheel mechanic. C-trailer license, but without a tendency toward competitive sport.

Andrea Henn-Gangnus

44 years old, diploma in librarianship, with a family of archers. Long interested in all textile techniques, and has learned and applied many (such as knitting, crocheting, patchwork, spinning and felting).

Ekkehard Höhn

Born 1967, training as an engineer and physiotherapist. Archer since 1972, plain bow since 1988.
Convinced that endless bowstrings are sturdy, reliable and reproducible.

Bernhard Hölzl

Born 1961, "About five years ago I was led astray by a dear friend into traditional archery. Since then, bows and arrows can no longer be thought out of my life.
"Inspired by beautiful self-made animals of the Egenhausener Bogenschuetzen, I got the idea if making targets for our club range out of foam sheets, as the store-bought 3-D animals are expensive and the club's funds are meager. In the winter, the foam animal targets show better preservation. Besides, they are easier to improve and enrich any archery range with their individual appearance."

Georg Klöss

Born 1937. Archer since 1999. Three years of recurve bows, then primitive bows.
Makes his own equipment, from the bowstring to the self-nock.

Authors and Artisans

Jürgen Knöll

Born 1964. Occupations: Toolmaker and data processer.
Interested in archery and woodwork since childhood.

Herbert Müller

"Born in 1963, but it took forty years until I came to traditional archery. Soon after that I began to make my own arrows.
"Curious and eager to experiment as I am, I soon tried the maximum in feather splicing: Arrows into whose feathers single bristles were worked. To make an optically balanced arrow, the cresting has to be suited to the colorful flags in the feather. My goal is creating this in perfect harmony."

Willi Müller

Age: 55. Studied pedagogy, for twenty years an independent weapon dealer. Thirty years of archery (B-trainer), many years as state trainer in the Westphalian Schuetzenbund. Author of *Arbeits- und Trainingshilfen fuer Schuetzen, jugend- und Uebungsleiter.*
Chairman of SV Marsberg e.V. since 1972 and initiator of the bow village and archery range in Marsberg.

Michael Prinz

51 years old, from Warburg, and he really owes it to his wife that he shoots a traditional bow. She was the one who called his attention to a Fita bow course at a People's School. Later a visit to a bow dealer got him interested in the tradition of shooting a longbow.

Then came building bows, arrows, quivers and experimenting with spine-values. Gradually the former Fita colleagues got interested in this different way of shooting. From the originally small group there grew the Sauerlaender Bogenschuetzen e.V. with over eighty members and their own shooting range.

Heinrich Prell

Born 1956, trained as an aircraft builder and carpenter, 20 years an independent furniture and product developer.

"I came to archery via bow building, after the first yew bow fell into my hands ten years ago. Snce 2000 I practice building wooden bows professionally and direct bow-building courses."

Stefan Schwed

Born 1962, electronic engineer for measuring and regulating technology. Through his interest in Native Americans he came to leatherwork and archery. For fifteen years he has been shooting a wooden bow and making leather accessories for himself and friends.

Literature to Take You Further

Leatherwork, tooling, leather plaiting

ABC's of Leatherwork
Tandy Leather Factory

Al Stohlman: Pictorial Carving Finesse
Tandy Leather Factory

Al Stohlman: Figure Carving Finesse
Tandy Leather Factory

Lacing & Stitching for Leathercraft
Tandy Leather Factory (catalog & orders via www.tandyleather.com)

Bruce Grant: Leather Braiding
Cornell Maritime Press, Centreville, Maryland
ISBN 0-87033-039-X

Beadwork

Peter Haug: Indianische Perlenarbeiten. Das deutsche Beadwork-Handbuch
Geschichte, Materialien, Techniken
Verlag fuer Amerikanistik
ISBN 3-924696-27-6

Felting

Gunilla Pateau Sjoeberg: Filzen. Alte Tradition—modernes Handwerk
Verlag Paul Haupt
ISBN 3-258-06166-1

Arrows

Ekkehard Höhn & Karl-Heinz Höernig: Traditionell Tunen. Feinabstimmung von Langbogen
und Recurve
 Verlag Angelika Hoernig
ISBN 978-3-9805877-1-6

Hilary Greenland: Praktisches Handbuch für traditionelle Bogenschuetzen
Verlag Angelika Hoernig
ISBN 978-3-9805877-0-9

Bow and Arrow building

Various Authors: Die Bibel des traditionellen Bogenbaus   Volume 1: ISBN 978-3-9808743-2-8
Volume 2: ISBN 978-3-9808743-5-9
Volume 3: ISBN 978-3-9808743-9-7

Verlag Angelika Hörnig

Various Authors: Das Bogenbauer-Buch, Europaeischer Bogenbau von der Steinzeit bis heute
Verlag Angelika Hörnig
ISBN 978-3-9805877-7-8
[English edition published by Schiffer Publishing Ltd.]

Magazine TRADITIONELL BOGENSCHIESSEN, published quarterly by Verlag Angelika Hörnig.
ISSN 1432-4954. Published to date and available: 44 issues with many self-building directions on the subjects of arrows, bows and accessories.

Knives and Knife Blades

Ernst G. Siebenreicher-Hellwig: Messermachen
Kosmos Verlag
ISBN 978-3-932848254

Bo Bergman: Kleines Brevier vom Messermachen
Verlag Th. Schaefer
ISBN 978-3-87870-861-2

Bo Bergman: Schweden-Messer. Griffe und Scheiden selbst gemacht
Verlag Th. Schaefer
ISBN 3-88746-402-8

Bo Bergman: Messer-Scheiden selbst gemacht
Verlag Th. Schaefer
ISBN 3-87870-676-6

Havard Bergland: Messer schmieden
Verlag Th. Schaefer, Hannover
ISBN 3-87870-661-8

English Units of Measure

English units of measure are usually used by archers. Thus bow, arrow and other lengths, including the fistmele, are given in inches, and the various arrow-shaft diameters in fractions of an inch. The pulling weight of a bow is given in pounds (lb.) and the arrow and arrowhead weights in grains.

The most commonly used measures and their conversions at a glance:

Measures of Length

1 inch (in.)   = 2.54 cm
1 foot (ft.)   = 30.48 cm
1 yard (yd.)   = 91.44 cm

Units of Weight

1 grain (gr.)   = 0.0648 gram
1 ounce (oz.)   = 28.35 g
1 pound (lb.)   = 453 g

Shaft Diameters

5/16″   = 7.93 mm
11/32″ = 8.73 mm
23/64″ = 9.13 mm

Arrowhead Weight

70 gr.   = 4.5 g
100 gr. = 6.5 g
125 gr. = 8.1 g
145 gr. = 9.4 g

Information on the bow

If a number stands on the lower limb of a bow, for example:

68″ and 50#@28″

this means that the bow is 68 inches long (= 172.7 cm, measured from groove to groove) and a pulling weight of 50 pounds (= 22.65 kg) at a drawing length of 28 inches (= 71.1 cm).

Arrow Speed

This is measured in fps (feet per second).
The value in fps times 1.09728 gives the speed in kph.

Notes

US $34.99

ISBN: 978-0-7643-3035-3